THE EMPLOYER'S GUIDE

Joanna Walker

WILLIAM M. MERCER FRASER LIMITED

© 1992 Age Concern England and
the Pre-Retirement Association of
Great Britain and Northern Ireland

Published by Age Concern England
1268 London Road
London SW16 4ER

Co-published by the
Pre-Retirement Association
Nodus Centre
University Campus
Guildford
Surrey GU2 5RX

Editorial Claire Llewelyn, Marion Peat
Design Eugenie Dodd
Production Marion Peat
Typesetting Joyce O'Shaughnessy
Printed by Bell & Bain Limited, Glasgow

A catalogue record for this book
is available from the British Library.

ISBN 0-86242-068-7

Contents

3 Putting plans into practice 39

4 Designing the programme 57

5 | *Delivering programmes: a practical guide*   86

About the author

Joanna Walker works jointly for the PRA and the University of Surrey, on a government-funded project to develop educational support services for pre-retirement educators throughout the UK. She has been responsible for building up the only national resource centre on pre-retirement education and is also involved in the production of various publications, including a national newsletter.

A former Information and Policy Officer at Age Concern England, Joanna Walker was a founder member of the Association for Educational Gerontology, of which she is now Honorary Secretary.

Acknowledgements

The Resources Unit of the Pre-Retirement Association would like to thank the following organisations and individuals for responding to our request for examples of good practice.

Aerostructures Hamble

Airedale Wharfedale College

Akhurst, Colin R (freelance)

A-L Pensions Services Limited

Barnardos

Blyth Associates

Bristol Folk House

British Museum

Co-Ed Consultants

Cooke & Burns (Personnel Services)

Devon County Council

Dorset Pre-Retirement Association

Dumfries & Galloway College of Technology

Dunstable College

Duveen, Pam (freelance)

ESTIC Enterprises

Fareham Tertiary College

Ford Motor Company UK

Gwent County Council

Gwent Pre-Retirement Council

Halton College of Further Education

Hyde Services

J Sainsbury plc

Leyland DAF

Manchester Business School

Mid Life Planning Associates

Money Management Council

MRC/ESRC Social & Applied Psychology Unit

National Pharmaceutical Association
Nelson & Colne College
Newark & Sherwood College
Nottingham & District Pre-Retirement Council
Options Pre-Retirement Services
Personnel Services
PREP Pre-Retirement Education Programmes
Provident Financial plc
Prudential Corporate Pensions
Reading Borough Council
Retirement Seminars
Riverside Health Education Unit
Rothwell Consultancy, Retirement Planning

Salisbury College of Technology
Scarborough Technical College
Scottish Health Service Common Services Agency
Southampton Technical College
Spelthorne Adult Education Institute
Stockport College of Further & Higher Education
University of Surrey
Walnut Tree Associates
Wiltshire County Council
Workers' Educational Association
Workers' Educational Association, North Wales
Workers' Educational Association, Thames & Solent

Acknowledgements are also due to: colleagues from the Centre for Health and Retirement Education, Tony Chiva and Allin Coleman; *The PRA's Manual of Pre-Retirement Education* and its author John Lumbard and editor Frank Glendenning; Stanley Parker and Chris Phillipson for research background material; Jenny Rogers, David James and the National Extension College for educational background material.

Acknowledgement of practical support is due to Michèle Bailey, Penny Searle, Mary Davies and other colleagues at the Pre-Retirement Association and the Department of Educational Studies at the University of Surrey.

Joanna Walker
April 1992

Sponsor's foreword

Better health, earlier retirement ages and better financial provision have done a lot to change attitudes towards retirement.

Once seen as a time of old age and shortage of money, retirement is now generally associated with more positive feelings: most of us can expect to spend a quarter of our lifespan in retirement and, with the resources to support a comfortable lifestyle, it can be a time of opportunity and fulfilment. However, lack of proper planning for retirement still leads to boredom, frustration and financial worries for many people.

A structured approach to pre-retirement education and post-retirement care can do an enormous amount to improve the lifestyle of retirers. As one of the leading independent providers of retirement counselling in the UK, Mercer Fraser has helped many employers to develop and implement pre-retirement programmes.

We are therefore very happy to lend our support to a much-needed guide that will be an invaluable aid to employers considering establishing pre-retirement programmes and a useful reminder for those who already have them.

David Taylor
William M Mercer Fraser Limited (A member of IMRO)

Introduction

A book for people who organise and plan pre-retirement preparation is long overdue. Both the Pre-Retirement Association and Age Concern receive a considerable number of enquiries requesting information about retirement and later life, and assistance with the task of helping people to prepare for retirement.

The willingness of managers to seek such help on behalf of their organisations reflects an increased interest in the people that make up company and business life. The human resources movement encourages greater consideration of personal needs within the corporate context, to the benefit of both individuals and organisations.

Older employees in particular have much to gain, and to give, by a better understanding of their role and needs. Retirement preparation, which is a much broader concept than attending a short course, is one way in which an employer can offer support and development to employees who have given of their experience and skills over many years.

A second reason for the increasing awareness of the needs of later life has been, simply, the greater numbers of people living into older age. All Western industrialised countries are experiencing the ageing of their populations, with all the implications for manpower planning, training and retraining, social security and services. Such changes will affect us all, and people of all ages need educational and practical experience to help them deal with the new situation. It is older people, perhaps, rather than younger ones, who are the pioneers in this particular revolution in the shape and values of society.

Employers and their organisations have traditionally played a key role in pre-retirement planning in this country, which began in the 1950s and 60s. The same pattern can be seen in America and in the rest of Europe. Educational services and voluntary organisations have now also become important partners in the field, adding their visions of what retirement preparation can offer to people in later life.

All would agree that good preparation involves more than attendance on a course or programme of events, and requires a combination of stimuli to encourage people to think about their future in a constructive and positive way. The pre-retirement course can play a pivotal part in this process, or it may be of lesser importance than, say, the effects of a good pension or personnel policy that supports employees through the transition to the new retirement lifestyle.

This book attempts to set pre-retirement preparation within this broader context, and considers the interrelated effects that different areas of company life and management functions have on retirement. To ensure that the views and experience of employers in these matters would inform the writing of *Preparing for Retirement: The employer's guide*, two important steps were taken.

Age Concern undertook extensive market research among its contacts and customers to discover what questions managers would like answered concerning retirement preparation. The Pre-Retirement Association asked its corporate membership for examples of real-life retirement policies, programmes, administrative systems, educational materials, means of evaluation and professional development, etc. It also undertook more wide-ranging enquiries through professional journals. The text draws on this valuable range of data, and some particular extracts have also been included as direct or further illustration.

The aim of this book is to give practical assistance to managers on these matters, based on an adequate understanding of the context of retirement today. The PRA and Age Concern believe that it will help meet a real need.

Joanna Walker
April 1992

An overview

of retirement

1

◼ What is retirement?

In the second half of the twentieth century, retirement has commonly been understood as the period of life after people have stopped full-time paid work, usually at 60 or 65 years of age. Until very recently retirement was considered as signalling the start of old age. What do most people now understand by the term 'retirement'?

Being old?

In today's industrialised countries, with thousands of people retiring each year aged between 50 and 60, the label 'elderly' is clearly inappropriate; yet this is the label used by the Government in its statistics. Many government policies rely on age-related criteria, of course, and without them, collective administration would be impossible. Official and social conventions regularly come up for public debate, however, and retirement ages are no exception. The issue of flexible retirement ages, with equal rights for men and women, has been under discussion for some years now, and official policy on state retirement pensions is now set to reflect more closely what has been going on within the occupational pension sector and in the retirement policies of organisations. Government thinking on these matters was published as a Discussion Paper in December 1991 (*Options for Equality in State Pension Age*, Department of Social Security, HMSO).

Not working or earning?

Retirement these days often means working and earning. It is widely accepted that the concept of retirement relates to a period in later life and a *change of major activity* (ie a different emphasis, rather than a total change), but there is a broad range of ages and stages at which retirement might start. It is important to remember that life-long, full-time employment followed by total retirement is not a pattern that everyone follows.

Recession and fundamental shifts in industry and commerce have altered the employment experience of many people now approaching retirement. These shifts affect both men and women, including full- and part-time workers and the self-employed, as well as the 'non-workers' at home, in the black economy or in voluntary jobs. For instance, a full-time employee may become a part-time, expenses-only volunteer. There is a change of emphasis: paid work ceases to be the main focus in life, and is now relegated to the relative importance of, perhaps, a hobby during the earlier years of employment.

Getting a pension?

Another characteristic of retirement is the change in source of financial support. However, not all retirees receive a pension (particularly early retirees and especially female ones), so this cannot be reliably included in a definition of retirement.

The difficulty of establishing a watertight definition of retirement was confirmed by L Bixby, an American researcher, when he observed: 'No single concept or measure of retirement is accepted either by gerontologists or policy makers ... it may relate to the extent or continuity of work or earnings ... to the termination of a specific career ... to receipt of a retirement pension or an individual's perception of this status, or to some combination of these factors.'

Society's need for retirement

So far we have identified key elements of a definition of retirement as an *age/stage of life*, a *change (of emphasis) in primary activity*, and a possible *change in source of financial support*. Indeed, it is society's changing ideas about what constitutes work, income, and an appropriate age for retirement that influence our ideas about retirement itself. Such ideas are directly linked to society's need to have more or less people in the labour market. Older workers, like women returners, are either wooed or squeezed out according to demand, and any retirement preparation needs to acknowledge that an individual's retirement situation is often produced by a conjunction of factors, mostly beyond his or her control, and is rarely related to individual characteristics, such as age or ability.

For example, in the late 1980s policy-makers and employers began to appreciate the manpower planning implications of our ageing population. The relative scarcity of younger workers seemed to signal an increased demand for women returners to the workforce and a slowing down of early retirement. In other words, mid-life and older workers would attract greater economic power, and policies to retain and retrain them would proliferate. However, the re-emergence of recession in the 1990s halted this development, and the trend towards earlier retirement and later-life redundancy continued unabated.

An understanding of the context for retirement will help retirement educators challenge any notions retirees may have about retirement indicating personal failure or inability. For the individual, retirement is just one more, albeit significant, stage in a life-long process; a process which insists we adapt to external forces and manage a period of change.

■ Understanding retirement

Researchers, educators and others who have thought about what constitutes retirement, especially in relation to the rest of life, have come up with a number of models. Although based on ideas rather than real-life situations, these can help retirement planning, because they aid our understanding of this phase of life.

The original model that dominated early thinking on retirement was that of the 'shock' or 'crisis', as the retiree fell into the unknown. This no longer reflects thinking about human development and learning, which is now seen as being life-long and continuous, rather than in defined segments. Furthermore, the third age is now a much better researched and understood phase of life, rather than a feared void — the period 'in God's waiting room'.

The following models are variations of current thinking about retirement, with the consequent retirement planning implications.

Retirement as a life-stage

This model illustrates the stages of life which most people experience.

THE STAGES OF LIFE: A MODEL

Phase 1	**Duration:** a quarter of life?
	Including: full-time school for all; further, higher, technical, professional education for some.
First major transition	**Focus:** EDUCATION/employment/leisure
Phase 2	**Duration:** half of life?
	Including: employment in some form for some or all of the period, of social and economic importance.
Second major transition	**Focus:** education/EMPLOYMENT/leisure
Phase 3	**Duration:** a quarter of life?
	Including: self-directed activities and roles, as circumstances and resources allow.
	Focus: education/employment/LEISURE

This model is, in effect, employment-centred, because the two transitions it highlights are firstly into adult life when employment becomes important, and secondly out of employment — into retirement — when activities other than employment predominate.

The strengths of this model are threefold. Firstly, the phases of life are not presented as watertight categories, containing *only* education, employment or leisure. Each phase contains all three but with differing emphases. Secondly, although the phases are chronological, they are not age-specific and do allow for flexibility. Thirdly, the model allows similarities to be seen between the phases, including the process of transition. The fundamental limitation of the model is its extreme simplicity. There are many other significant transitions in life, like adolescence and parenthood and, for some, dependency.

Retirement as a transition

Viewing retirement as a transition between different phases in life provides a rationale and an approach for retirement planning. It allows employers, and others who aspire to help 'build the bridge', to think in terms of anticipating and alleviating negative aspects of the transition, and of identifying and developing positive effects.

This approach represents a positive development from the old perception of retirement as a sudden shock, liable to cause psychological and other damage to the retiree, and for which all that could be offered was a crash course just before the traumatic event. The transitional model still appreciates that retirement may involve a loss of the inspiration and resources that employment ensures for many people. This is illustrated by the 'coping with change' model below.

COPING WITH CHANGE — A PATTERN OF TRANSITION

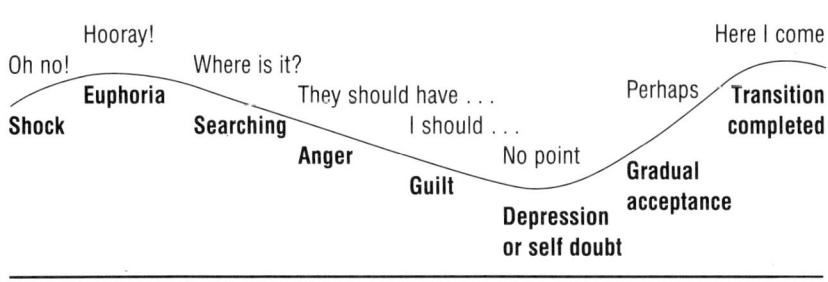

© CHRE 1991 Quoted with permission

Retirement as part of life's rich pattern

A slightly different approach is taken by those who have a more contextualised view of retirement, in which one's working life is but a series of strands or life-long 'careers' that are interwoven. The overall pattern may reveal dominant features at different phases. As in the model of life-stages (see p 18), education, employment and leisure each assumes a differing importance, but additional aspects are admitted. For example, many people have 'careers' in the domestic or caring domain, and so unpaid work intertwines with paid employment. There will also be 'careers' in health, housing, consumption, finance, leisure and so on.

The notion of these changing careers is important in providing for continuity and discontinuity. There is no general change from one state of being to another; a person may be in or out of employment, caring roles or education at any stage. As in a tapestry, therefore, retirement can be as abrupt as a discontinued thread in the employment 'career' or as gradual as a change in the overall pattern or hue.

LIFE-STRANDS MODEL

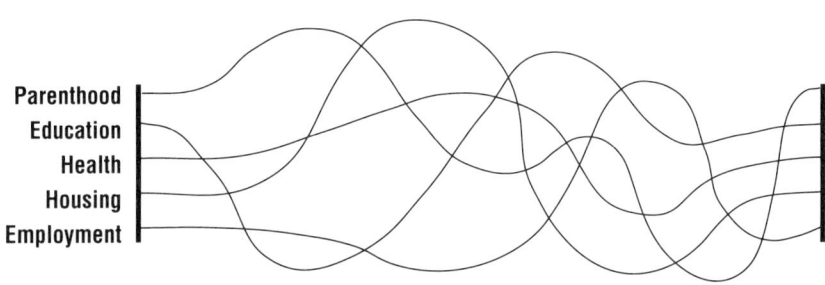

Parenthood
Education
Health
Housing
Employment

With this model, while not in conflict with the model of retirement as a transition, the implications are that retirement planning will concentrate less on assisting the transition process, and more on providing opportunity for life-review and personal stocktaking.

What do we know about retirement today?

There is no typical retiree. Retirement can result from a conjunction of external circumstances as well as from personal opportunity or choice. It may be faced by a diverse age range, comprising both genders, as well as different ethnic groups, occupational levels, and social and educational backgrounds. Each individual will have had a unique life-experience to date, and will possess a unique potential of knowledge, skill and aptitude for the future.

What sensible strategies can concerned employers and others adopt? How can they offer relevant opportunities to prepare for retirement, even when the timing and nature of the change may be uncertain? It may be helpful to know a little more about the diversity of those who are 'retired', and how they are perceived both by themselves and by society. Preparation usually involves knowing something of the way ahead, if not the details of the route or the final destination.

▌ The experience of retirement

There is little doubt that an individual's experience of retirement, be it positive or negative, is invariably related to the manner in which it begins. Two main factors are important: the individual's degree of control over the timing of retirement, and the acceptability of retirement, whether it is within personal control or not.

It is important to note that retirement is not just an event — it has duration. A brief review of a number of highly significant factors will indicate the diverse nature of this period of life, and suggest some useful pointers for planning. It will also provide a background against which managers can view their own retirees.

Numbers

What is the size and nature of the diverse group our pre-retirees are planning to join? Out of a current total population of just over 56 million, 18 per cent (or just over 10 million) are of pensionable age and over, constituting about a quarter of the adult population.

Although the *length* of life that people today may expect has not increased significantly in recent years, there have been gains in *life expectancy* as a result of greater numbers actually living out their 'natural span'. For the first time, society has substantial numbers of people in the post-parenting, post-work phase, with two or three decades of life ahead of them.

Another highly significant factor in any review of retirement is gender. Women make up the majority of retired people. By 75 years of age, women outnumber men 2:1. This may partly be a 'cohort' effect, as the current generations retiring reflect the impact of world war. However, over the century as a whole, women's life expectancy has improved significantly more than men's, largely due to improvements in maternal health.

For the foreseeable future, women's expectations of retirement will continue to be longer than men's, with fewer resources (low or state-only pensions), and with greater incidence of chronic illness in old age (over 75). Any preparation for retirement needs to take account of these factors in financial planning, action for health and lifestyle, housing, and anticipation of bereavement and single status.

Income and wealth

The levels of wealth that retirees possess have been the subject of debate in recent years. The general picture seems to be that although they are better off than previous generations, today's older people are not, comparatively, a wealthy group in society. Averaging their material status is particularly unhelpful since the retired population is composed of such disparate groups. In fact, the retired population represents the most polarised grouping of all when it comes to financial resources. There is a well-off group (comprising less than one-third) and a middle group, while the third and largest group is still living at or just above the poverty level, and reliant on state benefits. The majority do not yet benefit from the spread of occupational pensions, either because they had no access to such schemes, or because their membership records were short or scheme benefits modest. Many people still experience a dramatic drop in income at retirement, especially if overtime or bonus payments had boosted previous wages.

The inequalities that exist during working life are perpetuated, and even amplified, in retirement. Married people are better off than single people; men are better off than women; the young-old are better off than elderly people; single women are better off than widows. This hierarchy reflects differentials in people's work experience and earnings earlier in their life.

Financial planning for potential retirees requires a sensitive approach. The principles of money management may prove an acceptable context in which to discuss the relative merits of a range of financial strategies and services.

Educational background

It has been said that the generations currently in retirement, and those approaching it, have enjoyed very few educational opportunities and resources.

Initially, they missed out on post-16 and higher education because of armed service, and because expansion in these sectors did not occur until the 1960s and 1970s. Subsequently, as older workers, they have missed out on training opportunities which younger people can benefit from. This picture is borne out by the survey Social Trends (1991) which shows that only half of people aged over 55 have any post-16 qualification (men 57 per cent, women 40 per cent). Other age groups show levels of 70 to 80 per cent.

Older people do form a significant user group of adult education services, but they tend to favour leisure-oriented rather than vocational classes. This division is increasingly being used to decide levels of funding for local courses, with the consequence that older adults' leisure learning may be less available in the future.

Ethnic minority communities

Although the age profile of black and ethnic minority communities is younger than the population as a whole, significant numbers of first and second generation minorities who came to Britain in the 1940s and 1950s are now reaching or facing retirement. Their retirement planning needs have yet to be widely considered. One exploratory paper which has attempted to define likely demand for such planning identifies a particular concern. Many who came to Britain to work had long-term plans to return to their country of origin. Retirement decisions therefore include the extra dimension of 'homecoming' and perhaps facing up to the practical difficulties of realising a long-held dream.

Even for those for whom return is not an issue, planning for retirement in a culture different from that of one's upbringing may imply different approaches to those the typical planning programme can offer. For instance, there is evidence that the actual idea of 'retirement' — of being an older person in society — may be quite different for some communities. The Western concept of retirement, with its emphasis on leisure, may differ strikingly from the life-long commitment to the work ethic of those from less developed, rural areas. The alienation and low status of older people in Western society is felt particularly acutely, in comparison to the position they are thought (or remembered) to have 'at home'. It is likely that roles in the community and extended family would be more limited here.

This section has attempted to provide a sketch of current retirement conditions and experiences on the most general level. More significant to retirement planning is how retirees themselves react to the circumstances they take into retirement, or in which they find themselves after retiring.

Successful retirement

Today's retirees are said to be younger, healthier and in better material circumstances than previous generations. These are generalisations, however, and must be supplemented by an understanding of how retirement is experienced by individuals. Since there is no 'average' retiree, researchers have attempted to formulate descriptions from people themselves. Putting these descriptive factors together, they have been able to identify the features that are more likely to make for a satisfactory retirement.

Health is strongly related to adaptation to retirement. Poor health is not necessarily an outcome of retirement, but may be a feature of it at some point.

Income in retirement is also strongly related to whether retirement is viewed negatively or positively.

Outlook of the pre-retiree can be important for a satisfactory retirement. A 'positive' outlook contains elements such as looking forward to retirement and a feeling of self-confidence about being retired.

Activity in retirement is a concept much valued by pre-retirement educators, and is generally believed to be of major importance for a satisfactory retirement.

From this summary it is evident that planning for health and income in retirement are top priorities. These are areas in which both retiree and employer have responsibilities, and which should be acknowledged and acted on much earlier in life than just prior to retirement. Employers can also play a role in enabling a 'positive outlook' to develop; for instance, by allowing as much flexibility over the retirement decision as possible, by creating a climate in which ex-employees are still valued and welcomed, and by providing opportunities for good retirement preparation. It is interesting to note that a person's status and occupational or educational achievements do not predict how likely he or she is to have a satisfactory retirement, except in so far as they are related to income and health.

■ Feelings about retirement

Below are some reported reactions to the question 'What is retirement?'.

Retirement	. . . is a piece of cake
	. . . is associated with early death
	. . . is not for women
	. . . turns men into household helpers
	. . . is for hobbies
	. . . is for successful people
	. . . is about receiving, not giving
	. . . is about giving, not receiving
	. . . is doing odd jobs
	. . . is about staying busy
	. . . is about filling time

Source Comfort Zones: Planning your future (a practical guide for retirement planning), E N Chapman, Crisp Publications, 1990

Myths, misconceptions and fears may all influence our feelings about retirement and the changes ahead. Coping with change at any time of life requires a degree of maturity and security that is not necessarily linked to age. Retirees may find it useful to reflect on how they handled other periods of major change in their lives, in order to give themselves confidence about their ability to cope.

For some, the break with an employment-dominated lifestyle is a dream, for others a nightmare. An initial honeymoon period may give way to dissatisfaction with the new routine; conversely, the trauma and difficulty of the transition period may resolve itself in a new and fulfilling chapter of life. While adjustment to retirement is repeatedly related to a positive attitude, a *realistic* outlook is possibly more valuable. Such an approach faces the imagined gains and losses of retirement, and acknowledges feelings about such changes. This need not be incompatible with generating enthusiasm for the future. Knowing oneself, one's strengths, weaknesses, skills — in short, the resources at one's disposal — is probably the most valuable asset that can be taken into retirement.

Feelings about retirement may be largely bound up with the imagined contrast between the employed and non-employed situation, rather than with retirement as a separate idea in itself. For example, everything that is disliked about the work situation may be perceived as a retirement 'gain'; similarly, everything valued and enjoyed about work may be seen as a loss. Feelings about freedom from work — the gains — are often summed up by people as 'independence'. Losses are more varied and complex, but can be summarised as financial, social or psychological.

Another process of adjustment is also taking place within the individual or family that is thinking about retiring. It is the longer-term adaptation known as 'ageing'. This is a dimension of the retirement transition that is rarely explored, perhaps because it seems to offer little of benefit to the immediate task of taking on a new lifestyle. Yet it contains important concerns for some, which may present themselves as difficulties around retirement time, or even as a refusal to engage in any preparation at all. Others may go through the motions of involvement in the preparation programme that is provided, but gain no real benefit.

These more fundamental concerns with self can be raised within a good pre-retirement programme, but may require the back-up facility of a counselling function. This is discussed more fully on pages 84–85.

2 Thinking about

pre-retirement planning

▌ The employer's contribution

Retirement is a passage from one lifestyle to another. Those who take the voyage seriously and do the right kind of planning usually have a smoother trip — and more fun when they arrive.

Source *Comfort Zones: Planning your future (a practical guide for retirement planning)*, E N Chapman, Crisp Publications, 1990

As we have seen, the retirement process is one that has been conceived, experienced and described in many different ways. Nowadays it is viewed as a transition with identifiable phases, or as a journey with a beginning and an end. Seen in such a light, preparation makes conceptual sense and holds out the promise of effective results. However, different views imply different approaches to the planning task. They encompass pre-retirement planning that is bigger in scale than a pre-retirement course; that is wider and more complex than any single range of opportunities or benefits an individual employer could hope to offer.

The history of preparation for retirement has shown that (in Western, developed nations at least) large companies and employers have been at the forefront. They were the first to identify the need for planning, mount experimental courses, put resources into research and development, sponsor employees to attend retirement programmes and train staff to deliver such programmes. No government money was put into developing or supporting pre-retirement preparation until 1979 when two major research projects were funded, at the conclusion of which the Government agreed in 1983 to grant-aid the Pre-Retirement Association (PRA) to develop experimental educational work alongside its existing activities.

Those employers who have taken innovative action have done so because they feel a responsibility towards the people from whose work they have benefitted during a life-long career. For such employers, the question has been less whether to offer pre-retirement preparation, but rather what kind of preparation was most appropriate. Which approach, from a range of possible preparatory activities, should an employer sensibly choose?

The PRA has formulated a useful device to help employers make this choice. It is called the *Catalogue of Relevant Activity* (CORA) and serves to set an employer's contribution to a retiree's preparation in a wider context. Using this model (see p 30), providers can consider which activities will be essential, desirable or suitable. It gives them a basis for deciding what part they can play.

To give an example of this approach, a conference group working on CORA suggested social intercourse, personal thought and reflection, acquisition of information and cultivation of mental and physical health as essential preparatory activities for all. Such aims inevitably suggested the following provision: some kind of course or series of events that allowed meeting and personal exchange to take place; suitable or specialised resource material to convey information efficiently; a realistic timescale for the programme which would allow for possible changes in attitude and behaviour on the part of the participants.

CATALOGUE OF RELEVANT ACTIVITY

Each person	As an individual or in a pair As a member of a small group As a member of a large group As a member of society
has needs which he/she and others must assess	To gain moral support To gain awareness To set goals and plans To gain relevant information and advice To grow in confidence and make decisions To reflect, clarifying ideas, evolving personal philosophies To become more secure and socially acceptable To gain self-respect and self-fulfilment To be prepared and to survive
for which various people	Family Friends Colleagues Others sharing experience PFR providers Experts
provide various opportunities	For thinking For talking For listening For seeing For contemplation and reflection For developing managing skills
by various means	Reading material Question and answer Interviews Discussion Counselling Talks and lectures Case studies Role play Via the media

Source *The PRA's Manual of Pre-Retirement Education*, J Lumbard *et al*, Pre-Retirement Association in cooperation with Choice Magazine Company, 1986

Managers are familiar with the discipline of developing aims and objectives for the work they do, and the provision of some kind of pre-retirement preparation should be no exception. An initial exploration of intent can grow into a more extensive statement. It may well start with a conviction of the need for, and value of, pre-retirement planning, and the enlisting of support from other members of the organisation. Appendices 1 and 2 (see pp 123, 127) show examples of company policies and procedures concerning retirement.

∎ Is retirement preparation really necessary?

Some employers may be asking themselves whether education for retirement is strictly necessary. Today's society, with occupational pensions and earlier retirement ages, has done away with the two major dreads of the past — becoming immediately poverty-stricken and old. While improved circumstances are not enjoyed universally, the growing numbers of the retired population visibly enjoying active and fulfilled lives may make some wonder if they need to supply help and support.

Employers holding such views should be in no doubt that pre-retirement education provides benefits for both employee and employer. The following arguments were supplied by a number of pre-retirement educators.

Benefits of preparation for the employee

- It provides a time and an opportunity to take stock and consider the future.
- It helps engender a more positive attitude to life after employment.
- It helps provide a framework for defining both short- and long-term priorities in line with personal objectives.
- It helps make, or inspires the intention to make, particular plans.
- It provides relevant information, or the means of discovering it.
- It helps identify the skills and resources that will be required for the 'third age'.

- It provides a source of expertise, including counselling, to be called on further if necessary.
- It provides an opportunity to explore feelings about retirement, preferably with one's partner if applicable.
- It provides an opportunity to share experiences with a group of people at a similar life-stage.
- It gives the chance to identify, confront and define solutions for particular fears and problems.

Costs of preparation to the employee
- It requires personal commitment, time and effort (and similar from one's partner, if present).
- It may involve a financial cost, if the employer is unwilling to sponsor an employee's attendance on a programme.

Benefits of preparation for the employer
- It gives reassurance and a sense of direction to older employees, with the possible consequence of improving morale and performance.
- It increases employee satisfaction, by sharing the sense of control over the retirement process.
- It increases employee knowledge and appreciation of the company pension and related employee benefits (which are relatively expensive to provide).
- It facilitates successful transitions before and after retirement, thus preserving a good working environment for the retirees' colleagues.
- It decreases the potential need for expensive individual employee counselling.
- It allows for more accurate and sympathetic succession/manpower planning.
- It gives a clearer picture of an employee's general plans where these might impinge on the company.

- It creates good relations with retired staff, enabling the option of re-engagement to assist for temporary or consultancy periods.
- It improves the company image as a caring employer both inside the organisation and in the community.

Costs of preparation to the employer

- There is the direct cost of organising, staffing, and running a pre-retirement programme in-house, or buying in consultancy or training services.
- Work time will be lost by those participating.
- There will be the usual overheads attributable to such activities, such as ongoing administration, planning, training resources, use and hire of premises, etc.

▌ Planning within company activities

In order to be a success, elements of preparation for retirement should be present throughout an employee's entire working life. An overall pre-retirement policy requires careful planning in three main areas of company activity:

Personnel and employee benefits

Training and staff development

Employee assistance and counselling

Personnel and employee benefits

Adequate financial resources are a vital prerequisite for successful retirement. The company pension package is without doubt a key area of pre-retirement policy. The terms and timing of the pension, and the degree of flexibility and choice on offer cannot be underestimated. An early pension package may well be the trigger for a retirement decision, and the consequent need for immediate pre-retirement education.

A personnel policy that is efficient, and tactfully keeps employees in touch with pre-retirement-related activities, choices and decisions contributes significantly to successful retirement planning. Conversely, personnel records that have difficulty providing much information beyond an employee's age and joining date will do little to assist a pre-retirement programme. The administration of employee information is one of the keys to success.

Training and staff development

These activities are widely regarded as an investment in human resources; indeed, they have been described as the only company assets which do not depreciate!

An example of incorporating elements of preparation for retirement into a training policy is provided by Ford Motor Company Ltd. The Ford Employee Development and Assistance Programme (EDAP) is a joint initiative by Ford and its trade unions. It offers support for employees to pursue many kinds of educational opportunities, from basic to higher academic qualifications, to vocational, health or interest-related programmes — all opportunities for personal growth. Active liaison with local educational institutions helps coordinate the supply and demand for courses. Educational counselling facilities are available to assist employees choose the right course, and where appropriate new courses are developed and run in-house. There is an additional focus on increasing employees' awareness of health issues, with special clinics, screening and personal advice. All such facilities are in addition to the normal company job-related training and occupational health services.

While not every employer can afford to provide such a range of facilities, the contribution that an existing or enhanced training policy makes to retirement preparation should not be overlooked.

An alternative means of staff development and pre-retirement experience, which has gained in popularity, is secondment, the arrangement whereby employees spend periods, normally up to two years, gaining and sharing experience in another organisation, funded by their employer. This offers advantages to all the concerned parties. Specialist agencies have been formed which help foster the concept of secondment and assist with placements, especially between business and community organisations such as charities. One such agency, the Action Resource Centre (address on p 113), promotes the value of secondment for middle- and later-life career development and pre-retirement personal growth.

Mid-career secondments can be a powerful tool for developing staff with management potential, for enhancing an individual's ability to cope with change, and for developing new skills and refreshing long-serving staff. These can be on a full- or part-time basis. Longer-term secondments (two months or more, usually full-time) can be used by the company as part of retirement or restructuring plans, and in career development generally. They have a special place in the pre-retirement period, when a secondment may last up to two years full-time. Such an experience for the pre-retiree, apart from being valuable in itself, can often form a bridge into a future community-based life, or into a new retirement 'career'.

Employee assistance and counselling

This area of a company's activities is emerging as a major part of the human resources movement, and has much to offer pre-retirement preparation. While training and staff development can provide a range of opportunities for group and individual discussion, individual employees will sometimes find aspects concerning their retirement problematic, and will need special help and support. A company's employee assistance facilities, together with counselling by the pre-retirement tutor, should give them the encouragement to accept special help or to seek support from another source. This is discussed in greater detail on pages 84–85.

■ The manager's role in introducing pre-retirement planning

Managers who wish to introduce pre-retirement planning into their organisation need first to engage the support of senior colleagues, preferably up to Board level. They may also gain valuable support and assistance from the involvement of trade unions. The company climate may already be right for this sort of development; alternatively, some ground preparation may be necessary. Either way, managers will need to make a good case for this use of company resources, and be clear about aims, objectives and expected outcomes.

The general thrust of such a case is that employees who feel more confident about their future, who are able to make informed choices, are likely to work more effectively. Some managers present the alternative option: anxious employees, with unexplored worries on their minds, are more likely to have accidents, go sick, give bad customer service, and so on. Viewed positively, pre-retirement preparation, like any form of training, gives people a greater understanding and aids their decision-making ability and performance.

Another major justification for company involvement in pre-retirement preparation is that it reflects well on the employer. Such provision is increasingly expected as part of a good employee benefits package. A company which is concerned for its image in the community, as well as for its employee care, will welcome pre- and post-retirement activities that enhance its local standing, such as pre-retirement secondments, release for voluntary work or educational pursuits, and a clear pre- and post-retirement policy and benefit structure.

Individual managers may feel resistance to the argument that pre-retirement preparation is a worthwhile activity for an employer because they are not convinced by its case, or perhaps because of ambivalent feelings about their own long-term future. Conversely, personal contact or experience may have alerted some managers to the value of preparation. They are then better able to convince colleagues and to enlist cooperation.

Much depends on a company's climate and its commitment to human resources. If the atmosphere is secure (in the sense that people know where they stand), challenging and supportive, and if communication is good, there will be less anxiety about introducing retirement preparation. If, however, the situation is less promising, responsibility for pre-retirement provision may be perceived as being the short straw that nobody wants, or even as the task that heralds one's own departure. Once integrated within a successful personnel training or employee benefit policy, however, managers report that responsibility for pre-retirement provision brings a great sense of achievement, commitment and satisfaction to its proponents, be they at a junior or senior level of management.

Managers who are convinced of the value of pre-retirement preparation cite employees' greater sense of confidence about the future, of their being able to make informed decisions and being less likely to feel resentful or worried. The sometimes-voiced managerial fear that encouraging thoughts about retirement will create anxieties in people, or make them lose interest in work, is unfounded.

Difficulties in the attitudes of some managers may be related to their views about older workers. They may feel that no-one over 40 can change or learn. They may be concerned that older employees will resent a younger person organising an activity that can be highly personal. Such managers need to be assured that older people can and do learn new information, skills and attitudes with the right atmosphere of encouragement and motivation.

Relating personally to older workers requires time, attention and respect. A paternalistic attitude which encourages dependence is clearly not helpful; but listening, empathising, helping people to find their own solutions, and knowing when particular difficulties require special help are the keys to a successful relationship. If there are more serious difficulties with a manager's attitude, which perhaps reveal an ageist approach to older people in the workplace, then these should be acknowledged. A more sympathetic individual will need to be appointed to the task of developing the pre-retirement work successfully.

Having made a good case, enlisted the support of colleagues and thought about the corporate context and activities into which retirement planning might fit, managers are now ready to consider in more detail how they might proceed.

Putting plans

into practice

▌ What kinds of preparation are there?

The provision of a formal course or programme of events is the most recognised form of pre-retirement support that organisations can offer employees. Such provision can range in scope from a relatively isolated one-day seminar to a programme running over a number of years. The buying-in of a pre-retirement preparation service from one of many agencies can be a substitute for the firm's own provision.

Organisations who wish to offer preparation for retirement should first discern the needs of their employees (clients, or members) and then gauge the particular contribution it would be best to make. This can be done in a variety of corporate contexts: training, counselling, employee benefits, welfare, etc.

Since retirement planning started in this country in the 1950s, courses have been mainly of two kinds — public or open courses arranged by the adult or further education services of local councils, and in-house courses arranged by larger companies for groups of employees. The typical formats have been a series of weekly meetings (perhaps lasting a half or whole term), or a one- to three-day event, respectively. In both cases, course content has usually been supplied by a number of presenters who have given talks on designated subjects thought to be of interest to retirees: health, finance, housing, contacts with people, interests and leisure, and a philosophy of life.

The longer course time which is available in the weekly course format is used by some colleges and adult centres to offer 'taster' sessions for a range of adult education activities, leisure opportunities, trips, visits and for the development of personal skills.

Although courses are still to be found in the two main sectors of public and private provision, a third dimension has entered the field. A range of agencies now supply pre-retirement planning on behalf of the employer who does not wish to allocate staff time to such purposes, or who calculates that a bought-in service might be more cost-effective. Such agencies will charge fees for their services and may be commercial (for profit) or voluntary (non-profit) in nature.

The current field of practitioners in pre-retirement planning, therefore, consists of colleges/adult centres, employers, and professional agencies.

There is a growing degree of overlap between such roles: for example, colleges may take on an agency role and provide in-house courses for local employers; employers may open their in-house courses to other companies' employees for a fee; some agencies, such as large insurance companies, may provide for their own employees approaching retirement.

There is also greater variety in course format these days, as a development from the old weekly meeting or two-day course formula. Although a programme or course consisting of a series of meetings is still the most popular form of pre-retirement planning, the length of such a programme may vary greatly. It may still be as little as one or two days, or may extend over a term of weekly, or a year of monthly workplace meetings. It may be part of an extensive staff development/human resource training programme extending over a number of years, or it may be specifically planned to start at mid-life and run up to retirement. Programmes may be residential or non-residential or may contain elements of both.

To these formats we should also add the possibilities that exist for distance-learning pre-retirement planning (eg the Open University course *Planning Retirement*), computer-based learning programmes and interactive video programmes. Those who are keen to apply the advances in education technology to pre-retirement preparation in a greater number of ways can see the value of home video and CD as future media. To date, computer-based and video programmes have necessarily been employer-based because of the hardware required.

Some pre-retirement educators have been wary of such developments because tutors set great store on the personal interaction that a face-to-face course provides. This has certainly been highly valuable in the retirement planning process, and the individualised learning provided by distance/high-tech methods in no way seeks to substitute for human interaction. Its main value lies in imparting manageable chunks of information, and allowing detailed pursuit of particular issues that are of interest to the individual working with the programme, usually at a time of that individual's choice. It is recognised that pre-retirement courses are not ideal vehicles for large amounts of detailed information, neither can they address every possible topic of concern to each course participant.

∎ Which course format?

To summarise this increasingly complex picture of formats, there follows a diagrammatic representation of today's choices.

Format	Short session, half or one day.
Learning style	Anything from fully didactic to fully interactive but requires specific and limited planning objectives.

Advantages	Low cost.
	Achievable objectives.
	Ideal as scene-setting for later course or for treatment of one topic/issue.
	Minimum staff release time required.
Disadvantages	Too limited time for full retirement course, especially if imparting information.
	If wrongly used can be unhelpful, creating rather than alleviating worries.
Suitable	For any size of organisation.
	For particular target groups of retirees with specific concerns, eg early retirees, mid-life financial planning.
	As pre/post course session.

Format	**Traditional short course, 2–4 days, non-residential**
Learning style	Anything from didactic to interactive, preferably with a mix of approaches.
Advantages	Fuller course coverage of issues and more discussion possible.
	Relatively low in cost, travel and staff time.
	Growth of 'group spirit' and concentration of effort.
	Effect extendable through pre- and post-course sessions and support materials.
Disadvantages	Often attempting and failing to be all things to all retirees, workable objectives required.
	Travel cost to centre required.
Suitable	For any size of organisation (small firms can send their few employees to local college/adult centre version).
	As end of working life 'crash course', if no prior planning available.

Format	**2–4 day course, residential**
Learning style	More opportunity for participation/interactive methods.
	Reflection and informal discussion possible between sessions.
	Mix of participants may be an issue, depending on methods used.

Advantages	Fuller coverage and discussion as with traditional format above. Greater group spirit and concentration if done well. Effect extendable as above. Definable 'time-out' from daily routine very effective for learning.
Disadvantages	Relatively expensive due to residential element and travel. Possible attendance difficulties if away from home. Concentration problems if contents/methods too heavy-handed.
Suitable	For organisations with (access to) suitable premises. As above, smaller numbers can be sponsored on 'outside' residential courses. As end of working life 'crash course', if necessary. Can be used as 'thank you' treat for retirees.
Format	**Traditional part-time course: half to one term series of meetings, regular workplace meetings over a period of weeks/months (fixed term).**
Learning style	As above, but with even greater opportunity to mix methods and approaches. Participants can engage in between-meeting preparation and project work.
Advantages	Usually relatively low cost, especially if catering element minimal or travel only local. Creates group spirit over the period. Enables maximum reflection between sessions, thus effective for learning. Effectiveness extendable if part of career-long training/ development programme.
Disadvantages	Greater staff release time required, though intermittent rather than concentrated period. Longer course time available may not be used to maximum effect, requires imaginative planning. College course may need supplementing with company-specific information.

Suitable	For organisations with (access to) suitable meeting space. Ideal where company can work with local college/adult education centre to plan and deliver tailor-made course.

Format	**Self-programming series of meetings (indefinite period)**
Learning style	Such programmes sometimes evolve from a short course where participants request facilities to continue meeting under their own direction, or it may be the chosen style of provision requiring only an initial session to start the process.
Advantages	Low cost, initial planning only by organisation. Relatively low staff-release time as meetings tend to be less frequent than with fixed period programmes. Content and style led by participants, so highly relevant.
Disadvantages	May eventually run out of direction/energy, requiring management help. May be too 'inexpert' for some. Participants dropping in and out of such a 'rolling' programme may not get adequate preparation.
Suitable	For any organisation with meeting space, and with company climate conducive to employee-led activities. May link in to post-retirement welfare services.

Format	**Mid-life/long-term planning programme**
Learning style	Can contain a mixed 'menu' of planning opportunities from mid-life onwards, including short courses, intermittent or one-off sessions on particular issues. Mix of methods and support activities.
Advantages	The ultimate in coverage, relevance and flexibility of provision for employees. Ability to cater for people joining/leaving organisation at various stages as well as particular groups of pre-retirees, eg women, early retirees, occupational/geographical groups.
Disadvantages	Could be relatively expensive depending on elements selected. More complex planning and administration, needs creative and careful designing.

Suitable	For medium to large organisations with employees approaching or in mid-age, especially if there is a retaining/retraining policy.

Format	**Open/distance programmed learning course**
Learning style	Learner selects time, pace and emphasis of his/her own learning, and sometimes own path through material. Can be based on printed materials, with/without assignments, tutorials or audio/visual elements. Can be high-tech, computer-based — though not needing prior computer experience, with/without video elements.
Advantages	Minimum managerial cost, beyond initial selection of learning package and monitoring usage. Minimal staff-release time (often allocated in periods or employees' own time). Learning individualised to each employee's needs. Ideal for issues requiring information to be fitted to particular circumstances or large amounts of information that can be absorbed in digestible chunks.
Disadvantages	Cost of packages varies from small to large, especially where hardware is involved. Packages cannot provide human interaction, so best used in conjunction with a course or as part of a larger programme.
Suitable	For organisations whose employees are distributed over a large area, organisations with few retirees. As an adjunct to courses/programmes. As a training tool for retirement educators. For organisations with appropriate technology (terminals, etc).

Format	**Conference/leisure learning holiday course**
Learning style	Medium to large course group usually requires high quality lectures/discussions, with a selection of workshops/seminars that participants can choose between. Visits and tours, a social programme and free time can also be built in.

Advantages	Like a good supermarket, a conference/holiday course has something for everyone because of its size! Length of course/residential element enables commitment and participation. Combines learning with leisure, usually an effective strategy. Individual sessions with 'experts' can be arranged.
Disadvantages	Possibly longer period of staff release. Style may not suit everyone. Residential element and travel mean relatively high cost, but many courses represent good value. Cost of organisers' travel if appropriate.
Suitable	For organisations with large numbers of retirees, and (access to) suitable venues. For any size of organisation that wishes to sponsor a few retirees on outside course. Can be used as 'thank you' treat.

Some special cases

It is worth noting that there may be other opportunities on offer within a company that have relevance to retirement preparation and adjustment. Interacting such activities with the programme to be offered will help generate a truly comprehensive retirement preparation package.

For instance, there may be policies and practice in the areas of phased retirement, late-career secondment, paid educational leave, sabbaticals and post-retirement work opportunities. While all such activities might play a useful role within an overall pre-retirement programme, the employees involved in them risk missing the retirement preparation, or some stage of it, or may feel differently in some way and decline to take part in it. As a consequence, they would be unavailable to discuss the 'transition' experiences the company has facilitated, to the considerable loss of their fellow pre-retirees who might learn from them. Such employees may require a more individualised approach or timing for the remainder of their preparation, which a traditional course might not be able to supply, but which a long-term programme could encompass.

A different problem may arise in companies where there is a policy of re-employment of past employees on part-time or consultancy contracts. In such cases, some likely candidates may confidently decline pre-retirement preparation because the end of work does not seem imminent.

They may later reach the end of their extended paid employment still without any preparation. Where would they then fit on the company's programme? This is another potential group to which pre-retirement planning must give adequate consideration.

■ Defining the challenge

Once all the options of current practice have been considered, the next step is to assess how best to cater for the appropriate individuals or groups. There are two major parts to this assessment:

Who is the preparation aimed at?

What is the nature of the task the company wishes to assume?

Who is the preparation aimed at?

To whom, within the company's staff, is the invitation to take part in preparation going to be offered? A general offer inviting self-selection is less likely to succeed in recruiting many takers than a planned internal 'marketing strategy' to defined groups. Below are some suggestions about groups and relevant programme options.

Target groups	Course options
Employees age 40+ age 50+	Mid-life planning. Early retirement. Outplacement/resettlement (to find further employment).
age 55-60 (or 60+)	Retirement planning.

Same age categories as above but particular occupational groupings, eg senior managers, white collar workers, blue collar workers	Particular groupings due to specific information needs, site locations, expectations or perceptions.
Early retirees/redundancy only	Groups with financial/employment issues in common.
Employees retired on medical grounds	Individualised or small group preparation, sometimes after the (early) retirement has taken place.
*Women only, in relevant age/occupational categories as above	Groups with life-course experiences and expectations in common (eg interrupted careers, lack of pensions).
*Single people (never or not currently married) in relevant categories as above	Preparation for single retirement lifestyle.
Ex-patriate retirement to original or different country	Groups with major personal location move/cultural readjustment related to retirement (eg from multi-national companies or members of black and ethnic communities planning to return to their homeland).

* These groups might be catered for within a more general or mixed course, by having separate sessions available.

What is the nature of the task?

What will your company be trying to achieve by offering preparation? The following questions may help your organisation to identify the kinds of preparation which would be appropriate. The questions prompt thinking on:

Policy

Planning

Participation

Policy

- What priority (and therefore possible resource) can be given to pre-retirement preparation in company planning, policy and practice?
- Does existing policy for preparation extend to all employees?
- Are employees aware and supportive of such a policy?
- At what age/career stage should planning be offered to employees, and who should be responsible for this service?
- Are staff records capable of identifying possible candidates for pre-retirement preparation at various stages? If not, how else can candidates be identified?
- Which management personnel should be involved, and at what stages?
- Should the managers receive training in planning retirement preparation, or in specific skills, such as tutoring, counselling, etc?
- How does retirement preparation policy relate to other staff benefits such as paid leave, travelling expenses and subsistence allowances for course attendance?
- If the company has an equal opportunities policy, how can its operation within retirement planning provision be ensured? If there is no such policy, how can managers ensure good practice in this regard?

Planning

- At what stage(s) can preparation be offered (eg 10, 5, 3 years/1 year/6 months before retirement)? What are the opportunities and constraints in respect of the timing?
- Would one course be adequate, especially if extended by pre- and post-course sessions? Does the situation merit the mixed-menu programme provision?
- What course formats and styles would best suit the nature of the employees/company or the community to which the majority will retire? (Beware of making assumptions!)
- How is the course content to be determined, and participants' requirements and interests discovered?

- If the course (or part of it) is to be run in-house, which members of staff have relevant skills/knowledge to contribute, and in what ways?

- From what external consultancies/agencies/individuals should advice and assistance be sought to supplement in-company expertise?

- Is course/meeting accommodation available and suitable? If not, where can it be obtained?

- What support materials should be available to aid the smooth running of the course and its educational value? Are these materials already available/capable of adaptation from national, local or existing company sources? If not, how can they best be created and supplied?

- Is it appropriate to run in-house courses? What alternatives are available, and how can these be assessed?

- What other local organisations could be approached to cooperate in a joint venture?

- What arrangements need to be made beforehand for evaluation?

- What are the possibilities for follow-up events/activities?

Participation

- How should staff be invited or informed of their eligibility to attend pre-retirement courses, with special regard to encouraging those who may have doubts or difficulties about attending? (See Appendix 3, pp 130–132)

- Is in-company communication effective? Does a positive climate exist that could promote the programme via ex-participants' personal recommendation?

- What is the ideal number of participants for a course (or elements of a course)?

- Will course members know each other, or will they have been brought together for the first time for this purpose only?

- Do the style and methods proposed for any particular course element suggest a mix of participants (ages, genders, occupational grades, work, locations, etc), or more homogeneous groupings (senior managers, women operatives, residential workers, etc)?

- Does the style/format of the course suggest, necessitate or rule out the attendance of partners? Would the presence of partners be appropriate at some stages, if not for the whole of the course?

- If partners are to be present, how are they to be assured that they may participate fully as course members in their own right? Is there to be any special consideration within the course of their views/needs as partners (eg a separate session, or a separate pre-/post-course questionnaire)?

- How can the participation rates of under-represented groups in the workforce (possibly members of black and ethnic communities, women, people with disabilities) be monitored and encouraged if unrepresentative? Does course style, format and content avoid racial, gender, class or other biases as far as possible?

▌Who will run the programme?

Once the ideas for programmes and some guidelines for their application have been considered, a choice needs to be made as to who will actually deliver the programme or course. Will it be run entirely using in-house staff and company facilities, or is there a case for involving outside providers of pre-retirement services, such as consultants, agencies and colleges? A comparative exercise on the merits and limitations of alternatives may be helpful.

There are three basic costing models:

1 *Employers may bear the costs of preparing and running an in-house course.*

2 *They may pay for employees' places and associated costs for attending an outside course.*

3 *They may pay an agency to prepare and run a course on the company's behalf, on-site or elsewhere.*

Of course, there may be variations on these basic types, combining contributions from the company and outside providers in different proportions. The following are some examples.

- The company uses its own premises and does the majority of the planning, administration, programme design, etc. It simply requires outside contributors to fulfil the planned activities.

- A college/adult centre helps with the planning and design, supplies some of the contributors to work alongside company personnel, provides the ongoing tutorial role, carries out an evaluation, on company premises or in a local hotel of their choosing.

- A local pre-retirement council plans, designs and staffs a course after negotiation with three local medium-sized companies which do not have enough employees at the target age/stage to merit in-house provision. A per head fee pays for a team of contributors and a coordinator, who run the course in a local adult centre or hotel.

The main factors in the decision whether to involve outsiders are *expertise* and *cost*. What combination will give the company the best quality provision (according to its policy aims in pre-retirement preparation) for the least outlay?

How to choose outside providers

It can be a daunting task to approach and assess consultants and agencies providing pre-retirement training programmes, particularly when this is a new area for your company. Below is a list of questions which will help you evaluate:

The people on offer

The package on offer

The people on offer

- What is the provider's general professional standing? Have they been recommended to you? How long have they been offering programmes?

- Are they members of appropriate professional bodies (eg financial, educational, counselling, training, etc)?

- What relevant experience or qualifications do their staff have for this work?

- Can they demonstrate the quality of their programmes through both testimonials and evaluation evidence? Will they allow you to observe them in action?

- Can they demonstrate competence in the training of adults, as well as in the subject matter of pre-retirement preparation?

- Do they regularly and normally evaluate their programmes, and develop their programmes accordingly?

- What means do they have for keeping abreast of retirement issues?

- If financial advice is to be part of the programme, is the provider (or any contributor used) demonstrably independent?

The package on offer

- How much responsibility for the total organisation will the provider accept?

- How much planning input/information will be required from your company? (If none, beware!)

- Is the proposed programme sufficiently flexible to take account of company/employee requirements?

- Does this flexibility extend to the style as well as the content of the programme (ie can it range from people-centred and reflective to topic-centred and instructional)?

- How does the provider intend to identify (preferably in advance) employees' interests/concerns/questions and how is it intended to address these?

- Are there options or different sessions available in the programme for sub-groups from the course group?

- Will the aims of the programme be made available to the participants before they attend? Are there any other pre-course materials or sessions to prepare participants?

- Is the proposed venue suitable, comfortable and accessible? Can special needs be catered for if appropriate (eg diets, disabilities)?

- Will the course/programme leader (tutor, chairperson) be present throughout the proceedings?

- If a team of contributors is to be coordinated by the provider, who will have the main responsibility for briefing and debriefing?

- Can the provider demonstrate that programme content is relevant to the proposed target audience, especially where it includes women as well as men, partners, single people, blacks, whites, early retirees, people retiring on medical grounds, etc?

- Are such minorities represented on the provider's course team, or are they all white, male, executive class?

- What size of group(s) does the provider recommend, given the number of course participants and the style/content of the proposed course?

- Can partners of retirees participate successfully in the proposed programme? Does the company climate allow for this on-site, or would off-site be better?

- Can the provider's package include any follow-up to the programme (eg materials, individual consultations, reunions)?

- How is evaluation of the programme to be effected for the company and/or the provider? What criteria for success does the provider use?

- How will the company communicate its satisfaction or otherwise with the provider's service?

Costing in-house and outside provision

Any breakdown of costs should be flexible enough to take account of the various combinations of in-house and outside expenses associated with pre-retirement provision. If an outside agency is levying a large fee for an extensive programme package including most of the planning and design, catering, course materials, contributors' fees, follow-up counselling, etc, then there should be few outstanding costs to be made to the company. Conversely, if the package fee is small, and does not include items such as contributors' travelling expenses, course accommodation or catering, the costs falling directly to the company will be correspondingly larger, as may be the indirect costs of management time.

Below is a checklist for estimating all likely costs: it is a vital tool in any costing exercise. (Please note that some of the items listed will apply to either the in-house *or* the outside provider column only.)

Cost element		Outside provider £	In-house provision £
Managerial time	Planning (policy-making, identifying targets, budgeting, etc)	————	————
	Delegating task (briefing, negotiating, etc)	————	————
	Monitoring delegated task	————	————
	Planning and assessing results of evaluation	————	————
DIRECT COST OF PROGRAMME			
Staff time	Course leader/team	————	————
	Course participation	————	————
Administration	Identifying possible participants	————	————
	Recruiting participants	————	————

	Producing information about participants for course provider	_____	_____
	Pre-course information, instructions, etc	_____	_____
Travel and subsistence	Course team	_____	_____
	Participants	_____	_____
Provider's course/ programme fee (can be group fee or 'per head')		_____	_____
Premises/room hire		_____	_____
Residential and catering	Course team	_____	_____
	Participants	_____	_____
Fees and expenses for contributors engaged by course provider		_____	_____
Course materials/ handouts		_____	_____
Follow-up	Materials	_____	_____
	Events	_____	_____
	Evaluation	_____	_____
	Administration	_____	_____

Designing the programme

4

■ Pitching your course: who is it for?

There are two main principles that should guide the first stages of designing a retirement preparation programme. One is to relate the programme to people's actual *interests and needs*, not to their assumed ones. The second is to pitch the programme at 'where people are', taking broad account of their prior *experience and understanding.*

These principles are closely related and following them should help produce a programme that meets participants' learning needs. This may seem an obvious point, but in practice some programmes fail to meet these basic criteria. There are many reasons for this, not least the pressure to produce a quick, low-cost and therefore standard course package. The alternative is not necessarily to plan a longer, more expensive programme, but to think and plan more imaginatively. It might even be helpful to 'role play' being a retiree (either on your own or with colleagues) and list the ideas, and concerns that come to mind. What would *you* want out of a retirement preparation programme?

Apart from reasons of cost, planners may have other difficulties in following the suggested principles. Some feel that such aims are worthy but unattainable goals. In some quarters they are still regarded as theory or jargon, put forward by those who wish to make a straightforward training task more complicated than it need be! However, retirement is not quite like other training tasks, although it does contain elements of training. In any case, for a training task to succeed, it needs either to discover, or to standardise, each trainee's starting point in relation to the skill it hopes to impart. With pre-retirement preparation there are many more dimensions to the training task than is usual, and arguably a much greater diversity among the trainees.

If pre-retirement preparation is not just a training task, it is not a 'briefing' exercise either although, again, it may contain elements of this. Retirees will certainly have information needs, but unless it is known with some accuracy what these are, the briefing may be inappropriate and wasted along with the opportunity to do something more meaningful.

Estimating the understanding and prior experience that prospective course participants bring to retirement preparation is difficult to do with any great accuracy. It is, however, a relevant factor in the design process of a course because it reveals much about people's 'preparedness to benefit' from a programme. Assessing 'where people are' may include an element of defining people's attitudes to retirement.

Three specific 'types' of pre-retirees have been observed by researchers.

The far-sighted have already done some thinking about retirement, realised the importance of planning, done some reading or learnt from the experience of friends, and are keen to know more and encourage others.

The joggers take life as it comes, are not reluctant to consider retirement, simply unaware of the need. They may or may not gain from retirement preparation, according to the quality of the programme and its ability to engage their interest.

The reluctant or antagonistic include the timid, the suspicious, the arrogant, the fearful, the unimaginative, the short-sighted, and the unjustified optimist. This group requires careful management! Those whose particular needs fall outside the scope of the programme will require other help. The organisation may be able to offer such support or suggest an alternative source.

People's work experience will differ in length and quality, and will have given them a great variety of skills, competencies, attitudes, etc. The role that work has played in their lives will also vary. Some accompanying partners on courses may have limited or no recent work experience. Educational attainment will vary, and some will have benefited from training or development either in the workplace, or in educational institutions. Pre-retirees will also be at different points in their understanding of themselves, and will have different personal styles, beliefs and values that guide their behaviour, including their retirement planning.

▌Getting a balance in design

If the traps of not knowing what people want nor where they are starting from are to be avoided, then an understanding of how pre-retirement preparation can help people is essential. There are three major dimensions to a retirement preparation programme:

The training dimension

The educational dimension

The developmental dimension

The training dimension

The programme can engage at the level of helping develop ways of coping with the immediate task of retiring. Helpful, timely information, and interaction with others in a similar situation may sharpen hazy plans, or turn preconceptions into more accurate expectations. This aspect of preparation has a training nature.

The educational dimension

The programme will also function as an opportunity to learn about retirement, to gain new knowledge and understanding about this stage that lies ahead. This educational dimension of preparation has several possible stages, and retirees will be entering the programme at different stages of understanding:

- realising the significance of retirement at a personal level;
- getting to grips with retirement issues (eg finance, health);
- realising that alternatives and decisions are involved;
- appreciating what extra knowledge and information will be needed;
- becoming aware of how to find and process such knowledge.

The developmental dimension

The programme may relate at a deeper level to the ongoing personal and philosophical growth that everyone is engaged in throughout life. The mental work of 'making sense of it all' will hopefully be helped by the programme, rather than hindered or left untouched by it. This is the self-development aspect of preparation.

Good programme design aims to help participants make progress along each of these dimensions — training, educational and developmental. In design terms, education precedes training, and it is these two dimensions which provide the basis for a 'core curriculum' for the pre-retirement programme. The training element is straightforward to organise and deliver, but may need to be kept in careful balance and not allowed to take on areas that are better designed as educational in nature. For example, a common fault is to train people for what we think their third phase of life will be. A retiree's understanding of his or her immediate and longer-term future is a personal affair, although the retirement educator may help to focus thinking. The developmental aspect of retirement preparation can also be included if care is taken with the methodologies employed. These will be discussed in more detail in Chapter 5.

The value of identifying the elements of training, education and development is not to segment the approach but to ensure that the different elements can be recognised and represented within any proposed programme. The challenge to the course designer is to produce an overall programme that will address education for and of the person and training for retirement.

A design that will work in all the ways discussed above is ideal because many people approach retirement not knowing how to retire. Some adopt a superficial confidence to disguise anxiety, and some pretend that retirement will not happen. Some feel that they need to work it out alone, while others have highly supportive relationships. Some experience a sort of bereavement or crisis due to their loss of a role, and need extended or individual help. Some have given thought to retirement, but have drawn inadequate conclusions, and view it as being solely about leisure. Others have reached an understanding that opportunity, challenge and chance are all involved but they now require practical direction.

Building on interests and needs

The interests and needs that people have as they approach retirement have been considered so far at a fairly abstract level. In practice every individual's actual needs and interests will be different. How can they be catered for?

There are a variety of ways to discover the needs and interests of those approaching retirement — for example, through a survey. Tactfully-worded items within a pre-course questionnaire will yield some clues, but if too intrusive may not be answered, and may even prejudice the return of the questionnaire itself. (See Appendix 4 on page 133 for an example of a pre-course questionnaire.) In a small organisation or target group, personal knowledge or a careful inspection of employees' records may fill in the general picture.

The following concerns, expressed by a group of pre-retirees, indicate the range of needs a pre-retirement programme may have to address.

Positive	Negative
I need to ...	*I need to avoid ...*
Establish a realistic approach to job loss, change of status.	Retiring too early or too late.
	A reduction in self-esteem.
Build replacement support structures previously found in employment.	Boredom, apathy or loneliness.
	Purposelessness, idleness.
Negotiate territory, security.	Ignoring or denying change.
Manage stress.	Underestimating the effect of retirement on partner, relatives, etc.
Enjoy better health and fitness.	
Find a new challenge and purpose.	Making mistakes in financial or legal matters.
'Give back' to society.	Moving/not moving house, if appropriate.
Adjust my priorities (eg spend more time with my family).	
Discover new talents.	Bad management of health/illness.
	Difficulties in relationships.
	Not coming to terms with ageing.
	Missing opportunities.

■ Planning the programme

Setting aims

It should now be a fairly straightforward task to set some overall aims for a pre-retirement preparation programme. Not only will such aims keep in focus your general purpose and design, they will also provide a standard against which to assess the programme's success. The following aims, which were provided by pre-retirement practitioners, serve as examples.

- To promote individuals' preparation for retirement in a continuity from mid-life, through the retirement transition, to life in retirement.

- To enable individuals and groups to build upon their life experience and philosophy, to present the potential of retirement as a life-stage, to help extend life-management skills and activities.
- To help people apply existing knowledge and skill to their own retirement circumstances.
- To give opportunity, assistance and information that will help towards the formation of personal plans and problem solving.
- To help manage the transition from employment to retirement.
- To gain insight, not to accumulate information.

Defining objectives

Aims are meant to be general in nature, representing an overall intention and direction. They will therefore usually embody an approach or philosophy that is the most appropriate or comfortable for your organisation. When setting objectives for a programme, however, more concrete ideas and outcomes need to be expressed. When reading through the above list of possible aims, the three strands of training, education and development can be seen as being mixed together in various ways. When proceeding to objectives, however, it may be easier to separate these elements since they usually relate to different kinds of programme outcomes.

The following are examples of objectives drawn from programme-planning processes, as documented by practitioners. They are grouped together according to their dimension:

Training objectives

Educational objectives

Developmental objectives

Training objectives

- Participants gain relevant information/knowledge about specific subject areas.
- Participants learn to improve skills in managing money, health, relationships, etc.

- Participants identify further information/skills they will need for retirement, and where/how to obtain them.
- Participants learn how to work on personal goal-setting and planning for retirement.

Educational objectives

- Participants increase their understanding of the processes involved in retirement transition and what it will mean for them.
- Participants develop awareness of their own strengths and limitations, as well as the opportunities and threats that present themselves at/around retirement.
- Participants interact with others in a group, contributing to and receiving from each other's experience of this life-stage.

Developmental objectives

- Participants reflect on their previous management of change at other times of life, and identify the values and other factors which determined their course of action.
- Participants clarify the importance of, and priorities within, current and prospective activities.
- Participants consider the motivations and meanings (and belief system if applicable) that will influence their goal-setting and planning for retirement.

It may seem a false division to pursue these different objectives separately, but a reasonable analogy is to view them as skeleton, muscle and flesh which together function interdependently to form the 'anatomy' of a programme. A particular limb can be studied to see how it works involving all three elements; or equally pertinently, the three constituents can be inspected to see how they contribute throughout the body.

As some suggestions for programme items that meet these objectives are made, a picture of the 'body' or programme should begin to take shape. Below is a chart that reviews the design process described so far, and which can be completed as your plans progress.

STEPS IN PROGRAMME DESIGN — A REVIEW

Interests and needs of target group(s)

_____

_____

_____

_____

Estimate of level(s) of prior understanding/experience of retirement issues

_____

_____

_____

_____

Aim(s) of programme

_____

_____

_____

_____

Objectives Training

_____

_____

_____

_____

Educational

_____

_____

_____

_____

Developmental

_____

_____

_____

_____

_____

Designing the content

Once aims and objectives have been identified, it is a relatively simple task to map out the detailed structure of a pre-retirement course. Careful planning at each stage will ensure that the course achieves your aims in the way you envisaged.

The following chart may assist in drawing up a draft plan. The questions review ideas discussed previously and preview some of the 'nuts and bolts' issues of running the course, to be described in the next chapter. It might be useful to use a blank version of the chart in which to write your own draft plan.

DRAFT COURSE PLAN

Context
Is this a course, workshop or seminar?

_____

Are there several periodical meetings or one/two main blocks?
Weekday or weekend? am or pm?

_____

_____

Aims
What are the overall purposes and aims (for both organisation and participant)?

_____

_____

Content
What topics/subjects/issues will best address the objectives you have identified?

_____

_____

_____

Ways of 'teaching'
What methods or activities will be appropriate for the group/issues to be covered?

_____

_____

_____

Sequence
Is there a best order in which to present the content according to your aims, resources, etc?

_____

_____

_____

Environment
What is needed for your purposes – premises, equipment, activities, etc?

_____

_____

_____

Putting it in order

The next stage is to divide the proposed content into workable sessions according to the time available. The sessions then need to be arranged in the most suitable order for the learning you plan to achieve. This involves analysing which elements of the course can be handled together, and working out a logical and practicable sequence. Sometimes a particular course may wish to emphasise a theme, such as finance or health, yet deal with many of the interrelated issues of retirement that will arise.

Having defined how many sessions your time-frame will admit, excluding refreshment and social breaks, you need to create an equivalent list of groupings of topics/issues. It is helpful to write these down on individual pieces of paper or index cards, ignoring the sequence at this point, but ensuring that each session contains enough material for its slot. Of course, if sessions are to be of unequal lengths of time, some attention to sequence will be necessary at this stage.

The facility to shuffle the potential sessions around helps to ensure that the overall design objectives can be met. Are the elements of skill development (training), increased understanding and knowledge (education) and/or attitudinal and personal understanding (development) all represented to the degree which you intended, or has the process broken down between the design and the content planning stage? If you feel the two stages are not sufficiently connected, your plan probably requires one or two adjustments. Consider an adjustment in the way the topics/subjects are to be handled. Consider also adjusting the list of 'concrete' topics (eg housing, welfare benefits, hobbies) in order to make the underlying issues more flexible (eg retirement living environment, sources of income, creative use of time).

A useful check might be to link your previously listed objectives with the draft course plan, before arranging the sessions in a proposed sequence.

Tops and tails

Timetabling decisions about how much course time needs to be spent on *introductions* and on *evaluation* need to be taken at this stage. Relevant factors in these decisions are highlighted by the following questions.

Introductions

- Do course members know each other already?
- Will partners (if applicable) know other course participants?

- What sort of atmosphere is it appropriate for the group to aim at (eg informal/formal but friendly)?
- Does the course start with refreshment/social activity enabling informal introductions to have already taken place?
- Would an 'icebreaker' activity be appropriate for the group? If so, how long would this take?

Evaluation

- Will course members be aware of the course aims and objectives before they arrive or will these need explaining?
- If group evaluation is to be conducted, when should this activity take place (eg near the end, mid-point and end)?
- Will pre- and post-course questionnaires be given to employees and partners?
- Is there to be a general concluding discussion that will also serve the purposes of evaluation?
- If evaluation forms are to be used, will time be needed to complete and hand them in before the course ends?

As is evident from the above, you can save time by distributing as much pre-course information as possible beforehand. This might include the course aims, objectives, outline programme; all administrative details concerning venue, course timetable, etc; the names of tutors, presenters and other delegates (along with any other details about them that are appropriate); any preparatory activities or hand-outs; evaluation form.

The consultation process

Having worked out a sequence for the proposed sessions, and added introductions and evaluation if required, the final stage is to firm up your draft course plan. How and when this is done will depend on how much you intend to share the planning process with others. Ideally you will have already involved colleagues, most importantly the person(s) who is/are to deliver the programme, be they part of your organisation or from an outside agency, consultancy or college.

At this draft programme stage you may also wish to involve the 'consumers', the people who are to attend the course. There are sound reasons for doing so, and some practical ones for not. Briefly, consulting participants will help ensure that the content reflects their interests and needs, and will significantly increase their commitment to the course and the effectiveness of their learning. It is recognised as good adult training practice. However, extra time and flexibility will be required of the planner. A range of contributors may need to be kept in mind, or given a further briefing once the programme is agreed. Taking participants' views to their logical conclusion may entail engaging no experts except those who can work in a totally responsive way to the group's requirements.

Negotiation — how much is a good thing?

The extent of participants' involvement in content planning can be seen as a continuum. Adopting the best position along it for your organisation will enable the best combination of learning effectiveness and practicality.

This process is known in adult education circles as *negotiating the curriculum* or *setting the agenda*. Where retirement preparation is offered as an adult education activity it is an ideal area for negotiation since it is a highly individual undertaking and need have no fixed curriculum.

To sum up this section, consider this statement from an adult education tutors' handbook.

'Negotiating your plan at the start of your course will help to motivate your students. You are not only tailoring it more precisely to their needs; you are involving them in the learning process. But how do you do this? The simple answer is — ask them about what they need and what they expect. In practice this might not be as easy as it sounds. Students sometimes expect the tutor to know their needs as if by magic — and then complain that the course wasn't quite what they wanted. Students often have very specific needs, but may be unable to articulate them (even to themselves). You can set your course off to a good start by ensuring that both you and your students declare your expectations and review how these relate to the course programme. One way of finding out what your students want from the course is by asking each student to talk to his or her neighbour about expectations for the course.'

Source *Tutor's Toolkit: An open learning resource for first time tutors*, R Napper and D Batchelor, National Extension College, 1989

Examples of course programmes are provided in Appendix 5 (see pp 136–138).

■ Staffing the programme

Selecting the right people

According to the style of pre-retirement preparation you have in mind for your organisation, you will probably be looking for some combination of the following to help put the programme into operation:

Manager/planner/coordinator

Chairperson

Tutor/counsellor

Speakers/lecturers/expert contributors

Selecting the best people for the various tasks will be a key factor in the programme's success. Listed below are some general pointers about the roles involved, and the characteristics and skills to be sought.

The manager/planner/coordinator requires an understanding of retirement as a stage in the life-course and in the careers of his or her employees. In particular, the role demands an ability to analyse potential retirees' and organisational needs, a vision for retirement preparation and its value and an ability to marshall and manage appropriate resources.

Skills required include managerial skills of analysis, synthesis, forward planning, presentation of ideas to gain support, evaluation, accountability, and team leadership.

The chairperson requires characteristics such as warmth and geniality, the ability to listen, establish rapport and generate confidence and group spirit.

Skills required include the ability to avoid bias and irrelevancies, to communicate the aims of the programme, to make practical arrangements, to ensure consideration of 'minority' interests within the group, to manage and control the operation of the programme and sum up a presentation or discussion.

The tutor/counsellor requires a thorough understanding of the retirement preparation context, such as an awareness of his or her own attitudes towards older people and to ageing; a familiarity with attitudes to ageing held by people in general, including older people themselves, and the impact of such attitudes on older people's lives; knowledge of the needs and concerns of older people, both now and in the future, and knowledge of services provided by a large range of agencies (governmental, voluntary, commercial, etc) in order to facilitate effective referrals.

Skills required include competent group management, an ability to conduct discussion, and the counselling skills of empathy, listening, and a non-judgemental approach.

The speaker/lecturer/expert contributor requires a comprehensive and up-to-date grasp of his or her area of expertise and an ability to communicate it flexibly as the situation demands. Enthusiasm, confidence and tolerance will be valuable assets.

Skills required include communication, organisational skills for teaching materials and methods, listening and responsiveness to group, self-appraisal and team work.

Training for providers

Until recently there have been few direct training courses for pre-retirement preparation providers. Managers, tutors, subject experts and counsellors have had to rely on applying their own professional training and experience to the pre-retirement context.

Indeed it is still the case that a provider's professional background continues to determine the basis for the continuing education and training that is at last becoming available.

Formal training
Short courses
These are available on the *tutor's role* (both introductory and for the more experienced tutor); *for the planner*, concerning policy and wider retirement issues; and on the *counselling role* within retirement preparation. Such courses are available mainly from the PRA (address on p115).

Pre-Retirement education is sometimes a topic in the short course programme of other organisations who have an interest in it in the context of their own field, eg The Industrial Society, RELATE.

At a local level, health education/promotion departments of health authorities sometimes focus on pre-retirement preparation as a training issue, as occasionally do branches of the Workers' Educational Association, trade unions, etc.

Tutors, planners and contributors to programmes may also identify short courses and conferences on *specific retirement issues and topics*, such as those offered by Age Concern England, nationally and regionally; by the PRA; by the British Association for Services to the Elderly; the Centre for Policy on Ageing and other 'ageing agencies' and by the Institute of Personnel Management, the National Institute of Adult Continuing Education, Workers' Educational Association, etc (see pp 113–115 for addresses).

One particular distance learning short course has been used by tutors and planners: *Planning Retirement*, Open University (Community Education Department). This eight-week course can also be followed by individual retirees.

Longer courses
Longer courses that train people to help others prepare for retirement are a very recent development.

Certificate level courses offer a more thorough education and training for planners/tutors/subject experts. The PRA in association with the University of Surrey (Department of Educational Studies) has just launched the first award-bearing course: *Certificate in Pre-Retirement Education and Planning* and another is being planned by Manchester University (Department of Extra-Mural Studies). It is hoped that distance-learning versions of these Certificates may be available within two years.

University Certificates of this kind are nowadays usually 'transferable' to another educational institution where they may be built on to obtain a Diploma or Masters level qualification in a related field (eg education or gerontology). Entry to the original Certificate is open (ie non-graduate) making it accessible to a wider range of people, who perhaps have professional experience rather than prior qualifications.

Progress to Diploma/Masters level study would be relevant for tutors/planners who wish for a more in-depth academic study of retirement education, and its theoretical bases (education and gerontology). Programmes would usually be one to two years long, full- or part-time. A number of higher education institutions now offer taught courses in these subjects, notably London University's Birkbeck College: *Diploma/Masters in Mid-Life Planning*, and *Cert/Dip/Masters in Gerontology*.

Other gerontology courses are now available in Aberdeen, Birmingham, Keele, Liverpool, Open University, Surrey, Age Concern Institute of Gerontology at Kings College, London.

Informal training

If time and resources do not permit attendance on a training course, there are other ways in which staff can be helped prepare for pre-retirement provision. For example, you might organise your own training experience by finding out about, and sitting in on, other pre-retirement programmes. There are a wide variety of different settings (eg companies, public authorities, colleges, community groups, etc), and it would be useful to talk through the planning and evaluation of such courses with their organisers.

You could take this process a stage further by having a consultation session with the PRA or one of its 40 local groups around the country. Such groups will help to plan and assess individual programmes. Alternatively, book a professional updating session at the PRA's Resources Unit in Guildford.

Another approach is to invite an experienced planner/presenter to comment on your plan and/or observe you in action. Much can be learned from talking through their assessment, which should be constructively critical! If you can bear it, arrange to be recorded on video and discuss the results with colleagues.

Finally, read relevant literature about retirement preparation and keep up-to-date with retirement issues through your normal professional and commercial sources (journals, newspapers, etc).

Briefing contributors to the programme

The briefing for anyone involved in presenting or operating the programme will probably consist of a clear communication of your aims and objectives and information about the course group, the venue and its facilities. There may be need of nothing further, since staff colleagues will be aware of what is required, and any outside professionals worth their salt should be able to deduce from aims and objectives how to focus their contribution. However, a 'belt and braces' approach has been found useful by some programme organisers, and no contributor should ever complain or feel insulted about being provided with too much information. For examples of briefings for course contributors, see Appendix 6 (pp 139–141).

■ Assessing effectiveness

It is vital to find out whether, and to what extent, your programme is meeting its aims and objectives. Are employees being effectively prepared for retirement? Are you providing a high quality course?

It is worth defining the features of a high quality course. The following suggestions were made by providers.

Poor quality course	High quality course
Inadequate administration.	Participants stimulated and enthused.
Insufficient planning.	
Bad signposting.	New skills gained.
Presenter(s) poorly briefed about course group.	New vision/insights developed.
	Clarity of purpose.
Poor audio-visual aids.	Enjoyment of learning experience.
Pre-course information unclear or misleading.	
Incompatibility within course groups.	Confidence-building — stretched not exhausted.
	Good ambience.
Poor value for money/time spent by employer.	Fruitful interaction between tutor/students and between student/student.
Tutor's knowledge/skills deficient.	Tutor confident in knowledge/skills.
Timetabling unworkable.	Audio-visuals that aided communication process.
Poor timekeeping by tutor/chairperson.	Good value to client company.

Different terms are used in different circles for assessing the quality of a course. Educators will be familiar with the term 'evaluation', business people on the other hand will recognise 'quality control'. In either case, the purpose is to make a judgement about the merit of a process or a product, not about persons or their performance.

Planning evaluation

The following model describes one evaluation process from beginning to end. Each step is expanded in the notes alongside.

EVALUATION PROCESS MODEL

1 | **Specify the participants, judgements, and decisions to be made.** | Who is going to participate in the evaluation exercise? Just the planner or tutor? Or the whole course group? On what lines is the course to be judged? Refer to aims/objectives but include other factors if possible.

2 | **Describe the information needed.** | What kinds of information will you wish/be able to collect (eg numbers participating, opinions expressed, extent of group/individual participation, etc)?

3 | **Locate and appraise information already available.** | Some information may already be available (eg numbers and characteristics of group members, their expressed interests, etc).

4 | **Decide when, how and from whom to obtain additional information.** | Any additional information required will need to be specially collected (eg observational data, opinions on course content, etc). Will an extra person be needed to do this? At what stage(s) in the course will the data be gathered?

5 | **Construct or select information gathering method.** | Key methods will be questionnaires, observations, interviews.

6 | **Gather information required and analyse.** | Remember to programme in appropriate time and personnel beforehand, and allow for analysis and report writing afterwards.

7 | **Interpret and document information.** | All methods of investigation have weaknesses. Interpret results within context and without bias.

8 | **Report information as appropriate.** | Presentation of report should be according to its purpose and its reader(s). Will this include the participants? Might their reading of it be a means of further feedback?

9 | **Utilise report in future planning.** | The difficult bit! Warning signs that you are not meeting objectives are a programme that does not change, and evaluation results that do not indicate change.

Asking the customer

The simplest and most direct form of evaluation is to ask course participants either orally or in written form whether they believe the course was effective. Bear in mind that asking about some aspects of the course (eg the relevance of the content, the skills of a particular presenter) may not yield a helpful response if done verbally, on the spot. Time for reflection and anonymity will ensure a more reasoned and honest comment.

When consulting participants in a written format, your approach can be fairly 'open' with a few wide-ranging questions, or more tightly structured, requiring specific responses. The more open-ended the questions, the greater the variety and, possibly, quality of information gained. Analysing the responses will take longer, however. An open-ended set of questions might include the following:

- Identify at least three things that you gained from this course and will put into practice outside the course.

- If you were to describe this course to an interested acquaintance, what would you say?

- What improvements would you suggest for future courses?

More pre-set questions will enable a simpler, quicker collation of responses, but the breadth and relevance of your findings will depend entirely on your thinking to ask the right questions beforehand. A large number of specific questions with pre-set alternatives as responses may be suitable for computer analysis.

An example of a post-course questionnaire is provided in Appendix 7 (see pp 142–143).

Other forms of evaluation, besides canvassing the views of course participants, include the following:

- Observation of the course by a researcher, with agreed terms of reference for the research set out beforehand.

- Customer satisfaction — the 'word of mouth' recommendation or criticism concerning the course. How can this be measured?

- Assessing participants' learning. Both pre- and post-course assessments of some kind would be required, to allow comparisons to be made.
- Outcomes from the course, possibly in terms of project work (if applicable), action plans, or some other specific course outcomes reported by participants.

Evaluation concentrates on discovering the effectiveness of a programme in delivering what its designers intended, and so is an important part of overall programme planning and design. The larger context from which the programme emerges and in which it plays a part, however, may or may not be part of evaluation.

Quality control

Quality control is a broader concept than evaluation — which is seen as just one part of a three-part mechanism for ensuring quality. The stages in quality control are:

Monitoring

Evaluation

Review

Monitoring is the continuing collection, collation and interpretation of information throughout the whole process of planning a course (eg market research, course design, curriculum planning, costing, promotion, course delivery, administration, evaluation).

Questions to be asked include the following:

- Has adequate training-needs analysis been carried out?
- Is the lead-time to course delivery long enough?
- Are objectives being pursued right through to the follow-up stage(s) after a course?

Evaluation is the judgement of a course's value in terms of its organisation, content, learning methods, learning resources, level of guidance/support, relevance of aims and objectives.

Formative evaluation (made during the course) contributes to the learning process, as early feedback on effectiveness can enable adjustments to be made. The summative evaluation (made at the end of a course programme) tells how 'things could have been better' and will be a greater help to the next course than the present one. Data gathered can be descriptive and subjective as well as factual or statistical.

Questions to be asked include the following:

- What do I think of the course so far?
- Is it doing what it was designed to do?
- Is it providing what I/others want?
- Are participants learning new skills/competencies?
- Is it providing what the employer/client wanted?
- Is it being delivered in the right way?

Review is the final stage of bringing together the results of monitoring and evaluation. The course team summarises the marketing, organisation, design and delivery aspects of the programme (the 'input factors') together with assessments of the validity of the course (relevance, coherence), the acquisition of skills, and customer satisfaction (the 'output factors'). If the course is one of a series, patterns in results should be noted.

Questions to be asked include the following:

- Were interests and needs properly analysed?
- Was promotion to the right target group successful?
- Should we be providing this kind of course?
- Should we repeat or follow it up?

This method should, at the very least, help with future course planning. At best, it will indicate modifications that will improve cost-efficiency and course effectiveness. An additional recommendation is that, where possible, course participants should be involved in evaluation, and an example of one such approach is given opposite.

INVOLVING THE PARTICIPANTS:
ONE EVALUATIVE APPROACH

The evaluation is carried out at the end of the programme or a single part of it. It therefore cannot take into account post-programme evaluation, at 6 or 12 months, unless the course group is recalled.

Step 1   The course organisers (together with other facilitators) identify broad areas for evaluation, eg recruitment, the course programme, course methods and 'other comments'. More defined areas include pre-course information, accommodation/refreshments, course organisation, course content and course methods.

Step 2   The broad areas are presented to participants who may wish to add other areas.

Step 3   Each broad area is written at the top of a sheet of flipchart paper and two columns are drawn on the left-hand side of the sheets, one headed 'Strongly Agree' and the other 'Strongly Disagree'. (Participants are given these two choices only, as experience suggests that with more options or a 'Don't Know' column, people opt for the more neutral option.)

Step 4   Participants are then asked to write comments about each broad area of the course on small pieces of paper. For example, 'the food was too heavy' or 'lunch breaks were too short'. Participants can make as many comments as they wish about any area. These comments are gathered together anonymously and copied onto the respective flipchart sheets.

Step 5   Participants then take clean sheets of paper and copy onto them the comments listed on the flipchart sheets, area by area. Each comment is lined off from the next one. When this is complete, each participant has a complete record of the flipchart sheets and their evaluative statements.

Step 6   Individual participants then consider each comment in turn on each of the sheets and either tick the 'Strongly Agree' or 'Strongly Disagree' column.

Step 7   Once they are completed, the evaluation sheets are returned. The overall results are then considered by facilitators and participants.

This activity varies in duration depending on the number of participants, but will usually take 45–60 minutes. It has a number of benefits for both participants and organisers.

Benefits for participants:

- the comments are relatively anonymous;
- participants determine what is evaluated;
- participants retain power, and their ticks accumulate for particular comments;
- the results of the evaluation are clear and apparent and can be discussed;
- participants can see where their views are in relation to the views of others.

Benefits for course organisers:

- the whole course or any of its aspects can be evaluated;
- the feedback is a summation and therefore does not overemphasise any single view;
- more feedback can be obtained from the participants than by most other methods, such as questionnaires;
- the evaluation is available from all participants at the end of the course and clarity can be sought on any point.

∎ Ongoing support

The employer may wish to offer ongoing support to employees who have taken part in a programme of retirement preparation for a number of reasons. The programme may have succeeded in raising pre-retirees' awareness about retiring, and led to demands for further stages of preparation, or for more detail on particular aspects of planning. A different style of follow-on provision for the whole group may be appropriate to meet objectives that could not be provided for earlier.

Alternatively, it may become apparent that some individual needs have been uncovered, or have remained unmet, because a retirement preparation programme was not the appropriate support. These relate mainly to personal difficulties and problems, whether recent or longstanding. They may be intractable, or individuals may be helped immediately by the right agency, not necessarily the company.

Follow-on group activities

Where the demand for ongoing support can be met by further courses or programme stages, the decisions to be made can follow a similar pattern to that used in the early planning stages. Such provision may then begin to include participants at the point of retirement or actually even after it, if company policy is willing to resource such an extension. It may be, however, that other kinds of non-course activity could address some of the further needs and interests raised by retirement preparation.

For example, a self-programming group of (pre-) retirees might continue to meet and run their own activities, but draw (minimally) on company resources. Alternatively, a company post-retirement programme for its pensioners might be welcomed, with social and/or welfare dimensions (eg meetings, lunches, visiting schemes). The Employers' Retirement Association (ERA) can supply further examples, membership and contacts. Contact them at the address on page 114.

Individuals may be interested in arrangements for late-career sabbaticals, secondments, phased retirement, sponsored atten- dance on 'outside' courses, post-retirement work opportunities, etc, and a company may wish to respond positively to such initiatives. Additionally, a company may be able to provide guidance to help employees identify other courses (to be taken in their own time) which will enable them to pursue particular issues. Relevant distance-learning courses include *Planning Retirement* (Open University) and *Taking Stock — a Whole Life Review* (National Extension College).

Individual help

Where particular individual needs remain unmet, the manager will want to anticipate the nature and extent of support that the company might reasonably expect to offer. People may fail to benefit from pre-retirement preparation for a wide variety of reasons.

Some continue to have difficulties after pre-retirement preparation because they never quite grasp the issues involved, while others have difficulties because they have always coped badly with life-changes, retirement being no exception. Some individuals have little personal insight, and do not 'know themselves well enough'; others have suffered but not resolved a mid-life crisis, and this is brought back into focus through retirement.

Many pre-retirees find the ageing process difficult because of the increasing mismatch between their 'mental' age (how old they feel inside) and the way they are perceived by others on the basis of their physical age. Some find their powerlessness in the face of unavoidable retirement depressing, and others may have to cope with resentment from a spouse or children at home, either because of the loss of family income, or because of anticipated encroachment on their previous independence.

Finally, for many people there can be 'intimations of mortality' — a feeling of only limited years left — and the realisation of the gap between youthful aspirations and actual achievements.

Specific unhelpful attitudes include rigidity of thought, fear of failure, feelings of isolation and of being 'left behind' in a modern and changing world. In some cases these uncomfortable feelings actually manifest themselves in psychosomatic illnesses of various kinds, and 'retirement shock'. A few people, even when they have come to the point of knowing they need help, still cannot let go of such attitudes: 'I want help, but I'll make it as difficult as possible to be helped'.

Other general characteristics of the pre-retirement period relevant to a need for counselling are the 'bereavement' effect of job loss; the state of one's marriage and sexuality in later life; issues of singleness and loneliness. It can be argued that it is healthier for people to grow to know themselves better through the 'crisis' of retirement, even if this is a painful process.

In terms of preventative strategies, there are certain warning signs which give hints of potential difficulties in retirement. For example, is a retiree's occupational status of prime importance? Retirement, where in one sense everyone is equal, may lead to feelings of vulnerability. Those leaving occupations with high status or an element of 'vocation', and those leaving uniformed occupations may feel this most acutely.

Workaholics are another group who will have to find substitute activities for their current job, or suffer withdrawal symptoms. Obsessive personalities who need routines and rituals will find the disruption and potential void of retired life very threatening, and need to give close attention to time-management issues. Those who find others' ageist views of them hurtful will need to find a better way of dealing with such feelings than denial of the ageing process.

A major way of alleviating these difficulties is to provide individual counselling, using in-house facilities, or engaging outside resources. As employee assistance programmes become more common in Britain, counselling services for employees of all ages may already be available. Regular company counsellors may need to check that their practice encompasses the slightly different emphasis that older clients may require.

If counselling is not available, the company post-retirement prog-ramme may also play a part in informally supporting ex-employees. The skills and energies of the recently retired are often called on by such programmes to give individual help to their 'peers' who may not have made the transition as successfully, or who are exper-iencing difficulties associated with later life.

5 Delivering programmes: a practical guide

■ How adults learn

Learning is one of those terms that is widely used but difficult to define. Most educators agree that learning involves some sort of change in behaviour as a result of stimulus or experience. The kinds of change brought about by *learning* can be seen in levels of knowledge or skills, or shifts in attitude. By contrast, *teaching* is the creation of environments in which learning can occur.

Two general approaches to learning have influenced how children and adults have been taught, both in the past and today. Traditionally, the approach for all ages (including training) relied on rote-learning, which was considered to have succeeded when the learner could say and do the same as the teacher. A later, more progressive approach emphasised understanding, and the learner's success was seen in terms of the complexity of the problems he or she could solve.

Everyone can learn by rote, with varying degrees of success, but very little learning in everyday life is of this kind. Understanding or seeing meaning is a more important aspect of learning. Yet some tutors/lecturers neglect this obvious difference. A common problem of 'experts' who come to impart knowledge, especially to a non-expert group, is to assume that the audience will see the subject in the same way as they do. A logical exposition of the topic will not necessarily be meaningful to the learner, who needs to start from his or her own experience. If you apply this observation to the next presentation you hear on 'finance in retirement' for example, your assessment of such a session may well be different. Even concentrating on the principles rather than the facts may not be enough to link the subject matter to the understanding of the unfamiliar listener.

It is reasonable to argue that both approaches will have something to offer the adult learner. The tutor's problem is not whether to produce either rote or insightful learning, but to decide what is the best combination. This is why it is important to discover as far as possible pre-retirees' prior understanding of retirement. The tutor will then know what level of basic facts and skills need to be imparted (rote learning/practice) so that learners can acquire the basic competencies and vocabulary to participate in insightful learning, which must take place if participants are to make use of the course content as a whole. Moving on to the problem-solving stage will extend learners' basic competence through analysing and recognising the material presented. This must surely be a key aim of retirement preparation programmes. An overemphasis on rote learning with little understanding of the relevance of the material will not produce good preparation. At the other extreme, an over-emphasis on handling ideas with only a minimal level of competence in the subject areas involved will be equally frustrating for the novice.

The major differences between adults' and children's learning is adults' greater store of experience and understanding, and their ability to make meaningful links with new material. Since so much of everyday knowledge is involved in retirement preparation, a good course will often need to do little more than enable the analysing and reorganising process to take place.

Motivation to learn is another key area to be aware of with adults. They will be more highly but diversely motivated compared with younger learners. Their interests will be wider but at the same time they may be hampered by self-conciousness as learners. This may be especially true of older adults, or those who have not been in a recognised learning situation for many years. They are comparing their current self-image with that of an earlier stage in life, when they thought, felt and looked differently.

Little more needs to be said about the differences between adults and *older* adults as learners, since such factors as exist (and there are fewer than most people suppose) do not really come into play until much later in life (75+), beyond the age of retirement preparation. However, ageist attitudes towards people even in middle age are not uncommon, especially in the realms of job performance, development or promotion potential and even employability. Some retirement course participants may therefore be affected by other people's perceptions of them as incompetent, forgetful, etc. They will need help to boost their confidence and improve their self-image if they are to engage fully in the course.

∎ The role of leader

Discussing how adults learn has inevitably included some reference to how course leaders teach — using the definition of teaching as 'the creation of an environment in which learning can take place'. As the methods involved in this process are now considered in more detail, any reference to the 'teacher' will in practice refer to the tutor, lecturer, chairperson or whoever is leading the pre-retirement group at any given time. 'Teaching activities' will refer to techniques and methods that such a person will use.

In preparing to help adults learn — from their own experience, from each other, and from specialists — course group leaders will need to think about their own styles as 'teachers'. Most will teach as they themselves were taught unless they examine this assumption and decide whether or not this is the kind of teaching most likely to be effective for the current purpose.

Malcolm Knowles, an American educationist, is widely regarded as an authority on the role and approach of the teacher of adults. According to his precepts, the teacher of adults:

- exposes learners to new possibilities for self-fulfilment;
- helps learners identify life problems resulting from their learning needs;
- provides physical conditions conducive to adult learning;
- seeks to build relationships of trust and cooperation between learners;
- becomes a co-learner in the spirit of mutual enquiry;
- involves learners in a mutual process of formulating learning objectives;
- shares with learners potential methods to achieve those objectives;
- helps learners organise themselves to undertake their tasks;
- gears presentation of his/her own resources to the levels of the learners' experiences;
- involves learners in devising criteria and methods to measure progress;
- helps learners develop and apply self-evaluation procedures.

∎ Which teaching method?

In choosing teaching methods that will enable the teacher to function in these ways, it is helpful to refer to the objectives of the planned programme. The following guidelines are fairly crude, but they do indicate a range of teaching methods to cover the three dimensions of a programme identified earlier as training, educational and developmental.

- Where the programme has training (skills) objectives, the

following teaching methods could be employed: demonstration, discovery methods, work cards or handbooks, practical exercises.

- If the objectives to be met are educational (knowledge/ understanding), the methods employed could include: case studies, discovery methods, discussion, lectures, demonstration, private study, programmed instruction, projects, tutorials.

- The teaching methods which will best meet developmental (attitudinal/personal growth) objectives include: case studies, discussion, games, role play, simulation, tutorials.

The teacher's own preferences and abilities will also guide the choice. Some will not wish to lecture, preferring a more self-effacing style. For the 'cognitive' part of their course they will rely more on giving participants handouts or prepared reading, consolidated by group discussion; they may present short informal inputs as a lead into project work. Most, however, are capable of a range of teaching styles and move from one to another easily. A variety of methods within a course exploits everyone's sense of curiosity and interest, including that of the teacher. Variety is also essential because of the mixed nature of an adult group.

The essence of a teacher's problem is to transmit information, enable the practice of skills, and provide reassurance, guidance and activity so that each member of the group is learning throughout the programme. The point of the learning for the students is to enable them to carry on learning on their own behalf. However appropriate the methods or special aids selected, the success of a teacher will also depend upon the attitude and approach that comes over to the learners. If they receive the message that the teacher likes them, has their interests at heart and really wants them to learn, most groups will tolerate a less than perfect performance.

Giving a talk

This most frequently employed method of teaching can be used formally or informally in all sorts of settings, and with different sizes of audience. The basic pattern of communication remains the same. The lecturer presents the same information to each learner; passive listeners receive it individually and make of it what they can, but are usually free to ask questions at the end. The lecturer sets the pace, the content, the extent and order of the material to be presented. The talk may be illustrated with audio or visual aids.

Advantages

Talks are useful for conveying information to fairly large groups, especially if the presentation is factual and well organised. They provide a baseline of knowledge that enables a disparate group to move on together to further issues, or set a context within which later learning can be related. Talks may make good use of a teacher's skills in drama or oratory, and can be effective in generating enthusiasm and motivation.

Disadvantages

Most of the disadvantages relate to the one-way nature of the communication. What individual listeners make of the presentation will depend on their past experience, those benefiting most being the ones with existing knowledge of the subject. The success of a talk is also heavily dependent on the skills of the presenter.

Talks are a poor method for changing attitudes, especially where feelings are involved; you may win the argument, but fail to persuade. Unless a question and answer opportunity is provided, no check on understanding is available. A difference of interpretation by individual participants may well be acceptable, but misunderstanding is not. Attention span for this method is reckoned to be about 20 minutes. Effectiveness can be further reduced by personal mannerisms and habits that distract (are you a caged lion, a tooth tapper, an ear stroker or a coin jingler?).

Conclusions and suggestions

- Use a talk or lecture only when it is most effective — to give basic information, outline approaches to issues, contrast strategies, explain sequences of ideas, etc.
- State your purpose at the beginning.

- Present material as clearly and unambiguously as possible.

- Always include a question and answer section as a check on understanding.

- Keep to a maximum of 20 minutes, or break up longer presentations with other activities. Otherwise expect only the first and last 10 minutes of a longer session to be attended to.

- Be alert to signs from the group revealing boredom or restlessness. Be prepared to move on to another section of your prepared material or elicit questions or comment from the audience to discover any problems.

- Attention and interest can be sustained by the use of audio or visual aids.

- Note-taking is not usually expected in a pre-retirement course, so distribute a summary of your talk at the beginning (making annotation possible as you speak) or at the end for reflection or further reference.

- Avoid jargon, and be prepared to explain technical terms if they are unavoidable.

- Make sure that your communication is being received — check your audibility, the visibility of illustrations, etc. Be aware of special needs (eg for lip-reading).

- Eliminate distracting mannerisms, whilst retaining a lively appearance. Eye contact with as much of the audience as possible is helpful, as is the use of gesture, pauses and variety in voice tone.

- Any extra activities within the session that can enable the group to use or apply the new material will improve your lecture's effectiveness.

- Test any equipment to be used before the session, in the room to be used, and have a 'fail safe' plan (spare bulbs available, etc).

As with all teaching, the secret of a good lecture is exacting preparation. The following checklist makes all the key points.

CHECKLIST ON PLANNING A LECTURE

Objectives Make them clear in your own mind.
Make them clear to your students.

Timing Start and finish promptly.

The room Alter ventilation, heating, lighting and seating if necessary, and know how to do this before starting!

Beginning Make it vivid. Adult students, particularly, need arousal of interest.

Content Use the lecture for material that cannot be more easily read in a book. Keep to the main points. Keep it interesting and vivid. Keep examples/slides/overheads simple.

Organisation Plan a beginning, middle and end. Share these with the group by outlining your main points and objectives at the start; tell the students as you reach these points in the lecture itself. Summarise at the end.

Audio and visual aids Use them where they make a point better than it could be made verbally. Be careful not to obscure your own visual aids. Use large clear writing on overhead projectors and boards. Prepare as much of this in advance as you can. Leave illustrations long enough for everyone to see or read them. Adjust volume and tone on tape recorders, television sets, film projectors. Set up your equipment in advance; make sure it is working before the students arrive.

Duplicated summaries and hand-outs Keep them brief and attractive to read. Make sure that summaries represent what you say in your lecture. Use prepared notes to give references to books, addresses, dates.

Manner Be informal, responsive.
Speak up, ask if people can hear you, vary your tone and pace, control distracting mannerisms.

Evaluation and consolidation Plan ways of finding out how much the students have absorbed; offer them ways of consolidating and using the knowledge — eg discussion, role play, writing, multiple-choice quizzes.

Question and answer sessions

Traditionally, questions and answers come at the end of a lecture or talk. However, some members of the group may get confused during the opening minutes of the talk and then have to wait until the end before seeking clarification. Consider adopting something like the following three-part scheme:

1 At the outset, make it clear that questions are welcome at any time.

2 During the talk, pause from time to time to ask if there are any questions.

3 At the end, allow plenty of time to deal with questions and comments at greater length.

After inviting questions, the speaker will usually attempt to answer the first question asked. However, it may be that in any group of questions some will be more relevant and of more general interest than others. It may be helpful to hear all potential questions before beginning to answer any of them. The order of answering can then be adjusted so that more basic or important issues are dealt with first and questions which go together can be combined so that one extended answer covers them all. Using a flipchart or board will help you to do this fairly.

The best answer is accurate, relevant and pleasantly worded. Here are some of the more common rules for dealing with questions from a group.

■ You do not lose face by admitting that you do not know an answer. Some questions do not necessarily demand an answer. If there are reasons for not answering a question, say so and move on.

■ There is often no single correct answer to a question. In such a case you can either give possible answers yourself, or involve the group by asking for suggestions, confining your role to summarising these at the end.

■ Answers *during* a talk ideally should be brief and to the point or the flow of the talk will suffer. A question can be noted, if necessary, for later reference.

- A question and answer session can be spoiled if you are drawn into a dispute; it may be better to acknowledge the question or comment and offer to pursue it afterwards.

- Sometimes a question and answer session may begin to take on the characteristics of a discussion, and indeed it may be more natural to move directly into a discussion session.

- If the talk and questions and answers occupy the whole of a session, consider offering the group a typed summary of what you have said, along with some suggestions for following up the topics raised.

Using discussion

If a good lecture is unusual, so also is a well run discussion. Many pre-retirement courses advertised as discussion-based are in fact informal lectures during which questions and answers are exchanged. The teacher is still dominating the material presented, its order and content. This may be entirely appropriate for the programme concerned, but question and answer is not the same method of communication as discussion, although both rely on group participation and skilful leadership.

Discussion is where the teacher creates a situation in which students talk to and with each other freely, supplying information, asking questions, clarifying understandings, voicing opinions, working on group situations or statements. The teacher no longer dominates, comments on or judges the contributions, but exercises control through the structure and preparation that has gone into initiating the discussion. It is a more usable method than many suppose. In subject areas where there are no 'right' answers (eg what constitutes successful retirement?) it enables people to clarify their thoughts and feelings. Differing approaches to problem solving or skills (eg personal budgeting in retirement) are also amenable to discussion.

Advantages

Discussion is the prime means of participatory learning involving mental stimulation, challenge and motivation. It gives a context for individuals to experience a sense of themselves (skills, experience, values, etc) compared with others in a similar life-situation.

Discussion encourages many skills; for example, in listening, analysis, problem solving, reflection on and assimilation of information, and dealing with others' opinions. For teacher and participants it offers a means of checking, clarifying and extending understanding of the material.

Disadvantages

The nature of the discussion group — if highly diverse in prior understanding, personal circumstances, or from a strongly hierarchical work climate — may preclude successful discussion. Alternatively, the group may simply be too large for any discussion to work well. Occasionally, individuals within the group may be sufficiently disruptive or antagonistic to sabotage your discussion plans.

The physical surroundings may make discussion difficult or impossible (eg formal lecture halls, big draughty canteens, depressing low-quality environments, etc). Similarly, seating arrangements within the room can sometimes make or break the activity.

The worst group discussion scenario involves a teacher who has given up all responsibility for the learning process. Students end up talking about topics of which they are ignorant, in a futile and meandering manner.

Conclusions and suggestions

- Thorough preparation of the material, based on an earlier lecture, practical exercise or case study, will help group members to respond to the opportunities that discussion offers.

- Even where based on preparatory activity, the discussion task needs to take some account of the knowledge and experience of the group. It will soon run out of steam if relevant data or understanding cannot be applied.

- Some leaders set out a clear procedure or negotiate ground rules for discussion (eg sticking to the point, not interrupting, using the first person mode for statements — 'I think ...' rather than 'people say ...', no personal revelations, etc). Such guidelines should help alleviate anxieties about participating, and can be written up on a board or flipchart as a reminder.

- The best group size for discussion is between eight and twelve people. Larger groups can be split up once everyone is clear about purpose, procedures, etc. This enables easier participation for those who want it, and some encouragement for those who might otherwise stay silent.

- A seating arrangement whereby everyone can see and hear other group members will enhance participation through body language, etc, but also remember that sitting too far apart or too close together will not feel right and will inhibit.

- Resist the temptation to say too much, offer comment or evaluation, fill silences or correct mistakes; the main value of the exercise is to weigh ideas and conclusions.

- The group leader's responsibility should be maintained by encouraging contributions and ensuring equal opportunities throughout the discussion. Clarify or relate contributions to previous points and be ready to feed in or give sources for further information, if necessary.

- Remember, the informality of discussion applies only to the process as experienced by the learner; of the leader it demands as much planning and rigour as more formal approaches, if not more.

- The value of discussion is for course members to handle ideas actively, and to practise thinking skills to make the best future use of course material.

Using case studies

A case study can be used as the basis for a discussion, a spoken presentation, or for practical/project work. Its value is as a means by which course members can relate to each other and the issues involved. It can take the form of a story, or 'case notes' of a particular style, or be in the form of a problem. It can be written to be read privately, or acted out either live or on audio/video tape. The group study of a selection of facts, attitudes and difficulties, as represented in a 'case', provides a way for members to compare knowledge and approaches into more general retirement issues.

Advantages

Case studies are a flexible aid to learning, and encourage interest, commitment and responsibility for learning from group members. They introduce an element of real life into a course, encouraging participants to deal in specifics rather than generalities, and may even help to provide guidance to individuals who face situations similar to those that feature in a fictional case.

Case studies are useful in developing skills of listening, expressing ideas and applying principles to practical circumstances. Additionally, they give experience in group problem-solving, including the recognition that people reach conclusions and approach new events differently, and that more than one solution may be valid. Importantly, they enable shifts in attitude to take place without loss of face, after hearing others' contributions.

This personal dimension is very valuable. Case studies encourage recognition of one's strengths or weaknesses in areas of knowledge or approach, and allow a safe way for attitudes and feelings to be explored without direct personal reference.

Case studies on video or in dramatic form may have particular strength; playlets are available from Age Exchange Theatre Company (address on p 113).

Disadvantages

The main disadvantage is that case studies, of course, are not real life, and consequently any decision-making is without responsibility. This may lead to oversimplification or inappropriate conclusions.

If used in a discussion-based context, some course members may resent having to do the mental work involved. (This applies to all non-lecture methods.) Also, there will never be enough information provided in a case study for some people, who feel they cannot reach conclusions or solutions without more detail.

Proper preparation and presentation of case studies is vital, and a leader needs considerable skills to keep to the task yet refrain from influencing the outcome.

Conclusions and suggestions

- Be clear about the purpose(s) of the case study: is it to discover the relevance of issues which have been raised and to which more than one solution may apply; to learn decision-making skills; or to challenge or reinforce attitudes?

- Success is more likely with groups whose members have become acquainted with each other, and have some knowledge of the issues involved.

- It is important to ensure that there is adequate time (one hour or more for study and summary of conclusions) and space for small group work.

- If each group has a leader, be sure to have a briefing session beforehand, and if each group does not have a leader, then say clearly what is expected (ie that each group should formulate answers to the questions posed at the end of the case study and bring up any points they feel to be necessary).

Other group methods

The advantages and disadvantages of the methods listed below will be broadly similar to those for discussion or case study work. The need to do adequate preparation, possess good skills, and give careful consideration to the learning environment are vital for success.

Brainstorming

In brainstorming, a topic is introduced and the members of the group are asked to say anything related to that topic within an agreed time-limit of 10–15 minutes. It is a technique that produces volleys of ideas from a group in a short space of time.

During a brainstorming session, encourage participants to produce as many ideas as possible, either by free contribution or by going round the group (but with an option to 'pass'), and record all ideas on a blackboard or flipchart. People should build on the ideas of others, but do encourage free-thinking and 'far-out' ideas.

A vital rule is that no judgement or criticism should be allowed. This prevents fruitful ideas being lost just because someone shows disapproval.

When the brainstorm is finished, members are allowed to comment on any of the ideas. The quantity and variety of the ideas often result in a more creative discussion taking place than would otherwise have occurred.

Role play, simulation and games

Role play is a good way of giving group members an opportunity to experience a situation from another person's perspective, or to explore a situation which they have not experienced themselves. It is also a useful means of trying out different approaches to familiar situations.

Role play is successful in small groups or in pairs. (A third person might act as an uninvolved observer.) A situation is outlined and group members are assigned roles which they then act. They are given a brief which provides details of the characters they are to act and the situation they are in. The brief is usually written, but it can be spoken or in some situations may be worked out or modified through discussion.

Role play which is based on an emotional situation can be very realistic and even upsetting for participants, who may experience the feelings themselves via their role. Once the role play has finished, therefore, it is important to give participants the opportunity to talk through the experience of playing the role and allow them to settle back into their own identity. This is known as debriefing.

Simulation often involves elements of role play. With this method, the teacher involves the whole group in a more elaborate and complex problem, usually presented as a batch of papers (letters, memoranda, newspaper reports, photographs, forms), representing different aspects of a problem. Students can then either role play a meeting to discuss the problem or work on it alone, writing up a solution. Sometimes very small groups will discuss a report on the problem as if they were faced with it, but retaining their own identities.

Games are simulations with rules, winners, and often counters and points as well. They are an ideal means of showing systems or causes and effects at work.

- The teacher's role in all three methods is to prepare and introduce the material. He or she then steps aside completely for the 'playing out' stage, but watches and listens closely, only returning to an active role to conduct the final discussion.

- Keep your objectives clear when you use these methods, and communicate them to the group, in order to enhance confidence in the exercise.

- Make sure the simulation or game forms a part of on-going learning: prepare participants through lectures, discussion, reading, etc, and draw on the material it produces later in the course.

- The simulation or game should be as realistic and recognisable to the learners as possible. Decide whether playing imaginary roles, or playing themselves in new situations, would be most helpful to group members.

- Keep the briefing for the activity short and as free from unnecessary detail as possible.

- Ask for solutions to or evaluations of the simulated situations, in the form of a report or list of recommendations.

- Debriefing is probably the most important process in the whole exercise. Participants must evaluate, discuss, and re-think their activities, but back in their own situations. One important question always needs posing: are these solutions applicable to real life situations, and if not, why not?

Discovery methods and projects

Discovery learning is a term that can be applied in many circumstances. It is mentioned here because practical work, either individual or collaborative, is potentially useful for pre-retirement preparation. Enabling students to discover conclusions for themselves can be incorporated within several kinds of teaching activities: problem solving, group exercises, case studies and even programmed learning. Such an approach may teach skills as well as facts and principles.

Projects are a good means of encouraging resourcefulness, independence and enthusiasm where participants are asked to investigate an area of learning on their own, in pairs or in teams. They may make a genuine exploration into unknown territory, or they may do little more than reorganise the material to hand.

Both methods tap into the strength of learning by doing, which is so much more effective than learning by hearing or seeing. Not only is the outcome more likely to be retained, but the process of achieving the outcome will be valuable too (eg finding out how to gather pension entitlement data, and then constructing a real or hypothetical retirement budget). A few published sources of pre-retirement 'student' material, such as the Open University's *Planning Retirement*, have exercises that could be adapted for such purposes (see p 116). Project work, however, is possible only where a course has periodical meetings, rather than taking place in one block.

∎ The learning environment

The creation of an environment conducive to learning has been used as a definition of 'teaching'. An important part of this environment will be the physical surroundings in which the course operates. The room itself has been described as the single most ignored resource at a leader's disposal.

Everyday experience confirms how behaviour can be affected by surroundings; consider the different behaviour appropriate in churches, pubs, football matches, restaurants, doctors' or dentists' waiting rooms, etc. The signs we respond to are the scale of the building, the formality of its decor, our proximity to other people, the general comfort, lighting, and so on.

Arranging the course room(s) to suit your methods and objectives should not be neglected, and it is important that you have some say in the matter. Taking the room as you find it, or leaving course members to arrange themselves as they prefer, may not address your aims.

There are some common difficulties regarding physical factors. For example, an informal atmosphere is difficult to achieve in a large, bare room with a high ceiling. Similarly, discussion is barely possible between participants who are sitting in straight rows with a leader some distance away, and role play situations will be unconvincing if there is a lack of basic props (eg table, chairs, phone, etc).

By identifying the ways in which your surroundings will influence learning, you can engineer useful changes to maximum effect. In which ways do the furniture, the equipment, the room and the building help or hinder you as a leader? For example, the venue should be made as welcoming as possible, and be well signposted. It is important to be aware of the room temperature — is it too warm or too cold? Are the seats comfortable? Is there access for people with disabilities?

When you have identified the physical factors which could hinder the success of the session, you will be able to take action to ensure the best possible environment for the course participants.

The seating arrangements

Consider the following seat patterns in relation to what you are trying to achieve at different points in your course.

Lecture style	Leader stands behind desk, facing group in rows.
Question and answer style	Slightly less formal, leader moves to front of desk.
Group discussion style	Leader sits with group in circle.
Exercise style	Group arranged in pairs to work on a particular activity. Tutor distant but accessible.
Project or mini-discussion style	Groups work on (longer) project or problem. Tutor distant but accessible.
Presentation style	Similar in purpose to lecture style, capable of use with large group, but implying more participation (audience not in rows).

Needless to say, whichever scenario(s) you select during the operation of your course, careful attention should be given to visibility, audibility and special needs.

▮ Educational resources and technology

It is clear that the role of the course leader is a highly complex one. In addition to all the skills and attributes that have been described up to this point, the leader must aspire to be the greatest expert on the learning needs of the group. This is different from being an expert on a subject, and implies that he or she will know which are good sources of expertise that will be suitable for the learners. In other words the leader is acting as a resource.

If your lecturing skills are not your greatest asset, a video of someone who is a skilled exponent might take your place. You will know of other 'people-resources' who can be involved in the programme, either live or recorded, or whose expertise is embodied in written material. In addition, your own knowledge and understanding of retirement issues will be a resource for course members; you are available to them for queries, further references and contacts.

This concept of the tutor as *resource* is more challenging than that of the lecturer who makes good use of visual aids, as is the common perception of resource usage. When communication is more two-way, the 'resource-mindedness' of the tutor will be of great value. Good tutors will always be thinking of additional resources, audio-visual or otherwise, which can be handled by students as individuals or groups, and used directly by them for learning. Many of these resources are free or cheap and easily available. Their use is multiple: as direct information to be given to group members; as background or stimulus material for them to work on; as guidance material for the leader.

Which resources?

The raw material of educational resources is to be found all around us, from the personal and informal to the highly formal and externalised. The range is enormous, and even the limited list below will give some idea of the choice.

People	Print	Audio-visual
Commercial bodies	Books	Blackboard/flipchart
Educational advisors	Duplicated handouts	Video cassettes
Consultants and other specialised staff (eg librarians, museum curators)	Folders of documents	Films
Local people	Magazines	Film strips
Other teachers	Newspapers	Overhead projector transparencies
Professional associations	Posters and charts	Radio
Yourself	Programmed books	Records
Your students	Work cards	Slides and photos
		Audio cassettes
		Television
		Working models

In the past, a high value was placed on the 'expert', the official view, the facts. Yet in education for retirement, there needs to be an appropriate balance of training, education, and development. The fact that you do not yet need a certificate to retire rejects the necessity for a knowledge-based, expert-derived syllabus. Why not take a wide view of what counts as a resource for retirement preparation, and put high on your list of priorities the learner's ability to respond to and use such resources? You will then find yourself drawing on all kinds of information, systems of access, informal ways into networks, etc that are open to any diligent enquirer.

Preparation for retirement may not require large amounts of special information, but it does need a sensible and thoughtful arrangement of existing information that enables people to use it according to their needs. For instance, very little student resource material is tailor-made for the age and circumstances of people thinking about retirement. Even where material is said to be appropriate for retirement preparation, it may not fit all circumstances or it may be too generalised to be of particular use. Look at any of the so-called handbooks on retirement available in High Street bookshops and assess how much would actually help or interest you.

Most information or educational aids that are pertinent to an adult audience will be relevant to retirement preparation. As a provider, you are looking for resources that will help adults take stock, develop skills, stimulate thought and acquire relevant knowledge.

Using audio-visual aids

A teacher's purpose in using audio-visual aids (AVA) — for example, photopacks, tape, film, tape slides, an overhead projector or live recorded radio and TV — should always be clearly defined. AVA must support, not hinder. The reasons for using them may include the following:

- to illustrate;
- to summarise;
- to provoke discussion;

- to assist in interpreting data;
- to base an entire seminar upon relevant material (eg a television programme).

The use of AVA can make or break an event according to their relevance and the skill used in their application. A speaker who cannot use an overhead projector lacks a necessary skill. Badly or illegibly prepared transparencies adversely affect a group's motivation and a speaker's credibility. The use of such aids should be related to group size; for example, a video screen of the usual domestic proportions would be quite inadequate for a large group.

SUPPORT MATERIALS: A CHECKLIST

Tutor	Easels with flipcharts (two preferred). Felt-tip markers (several colours). Masking tape/blu-tack. Overhead projector and prepared transparencies (if needed) and pens. A blackboard (whiteboard) with chalk, markers and eraser. Audio-visual equipment as needed: VCR and monitor. Microphone. Slide/tape equipment. List of expected participants.
Each participant (at registration)	Pre-prepared name badge or place card or blank badge/card for participant to complete. A copy of any course materials. Paper for note-taking and pen/pencil. Programme schedule — listing times, locations, topics and names of presenters. List of course participants. Reprints of any articles of interest or relevant company publications.

■ Leadership and professionalism

It is important for all those involved in providing retirement preparation to judge how well they are doing their job. The evaluation of pre-retirement provision was discussed in Chapter 4. The other aspect of finding out how to improve provision is a personal assessment or appraisal of your own performance or practice.

Some may be confident in the feeling they get from a course group that they have 'got it right'. Knowing why would be additionally helpful. Some rely on the judgement of the market; 'we sell 70 courses a year so we must be doing OK' or 'we've had client X for 20 years, they always come back for more'. Again, knowing what it is that makes for such popularity would be useful, against the day when demand drops, or client X is offered more attractive terms by another provider. Such informal assessments represent an unexplored mix of approval for the product as well as the performance of the personnel.

How can providers' practice be assessed most helpfully, in order to lead to improvement and an extension of their knowledge and skills? As with the evaluation of the course, criteria need to be established, against which judgements can be made and compared over time or between practitioners.

A view of your professional strengths and weaknesses is a valuable starting point, and can be done by thoughtful self-assessment or by canvassing the opinions of others. Professional growth should be an aim for everyone, not just for those who are aware of having (or judged as having) difficulties or lack of experience. Assessment will help to identify areas in need of improvement and/or training.

Conducting self-assessment

Self-assessment is the easiest way of building on feelings you may have about the merits of your work. There are several ways in which you can gather evidence about your practice from your group members.

- Ask participants to fill out a questionnaire or comment sheet.
- Observe their behaviour and attitudes towards you.
- Ask for comment on particular aspects of your leadership or your teaching methods.

- Ask course participants questions to check *their* understanding and progress.
- Arrange to have yourself recorded on video, and scrutinise the results.

Collect further evidence from records you create, such as charts of levels of participation/flow of communication within the course group. Also, try making regular personal notes or a 'log' of activities and methods tried, and your expectations and feelings about their success.

If you are able to involve others in your appraisal, consider a fellow practitioner of similar or greater experience. Such an arrangement might enable mutual assessment. Sitting in on each other's sessions could allow for positive criticism to be exchanged in a highly supportive way. Again, criteria should be agreed beforehand, and can take the form of a structured checklist or informal notes. A video recording might be used as the basis of a discussion afterwards.

Another fairly neutral form of assessment might be supplied, at your request, by an observer or researcher who is not a teacher, but who is familiar with the theory and practice behind your work. Criteria will be pre-agreed, as before, and your observer should be willing to discuss findings in the form of an oral or written report.

Another dimension to appraisal comes into play if your assessor is not a disinterested party, but is in fact your employer, client, senior colleague or educational inspector, etc. In this situation, the criteria by which you are assessed may or may not be negotiable or even apparent, although there is good reason to request that they should at least be known to you. A structured assessment checklist of some kind may be used, or the report-back may take the wider form of a 'staff appraisal' approach, to include discussion of your own feelings and plans for development.

An example of a self-assessment questionnaire can be found in Appendix 8 and an example of a questionnaire to evaluate lectures is provided in Appendix 9 (see pp 144–147).

Professional development

An element in the report-back stage of any assessment process may be an identification of your further training needs. The training opportunities in pre-retirement education planning have been outlined on pages 73–75. The following list indicates other more general training courses available which will give basic or more advanced preparation for adult teaching.

- City and Guilds 730 Stage 1 (approximately 40 hours) and Stage 2 (approximately 130 hours) are certificates in teaching in further and adult education.

- ACSTT (Advisory Committee on the Supply and Training of Teachers) courses Stages 1, 2, and 3 are similar in purpose to those above and are run by local education authorities.

- Post-professional courses at some universities (Departments of Continuing Education) provide professionals who have a first degree in any discipline with a chance to study the teaching of adults at Diploma, Masters or Doctorate levels. A list of these Departments can be found in the annual yearbook of the National Institute of Adult Continuing Education (address on p 115).

- INSET (In-Service Education and Training) funding supports part-time local education authority staff to attend relevant courses and conferences elsewhere, or to visit other tutors.

Make enquiries of your employer, an adult/further education advisor or your local education authority's Staff Development or Training Officer about the kind of course that interests you.

Other possible sources of training are the professional associations in your subject area, which might provide courses which refresh, update or deepen your knowledge. Trades union education services and the professional bodies concerned with further, adult and community education (eg National Institute of Adult Continuing Education, Workers' Educational Association, etc) offer courses and conferences on a variety of topics.

Reading is another form of professional development and the following publications on how to improve your adult learning skills are particularly recommended.

- *Adult Learning, Adult Teaching*, John Daines and Brian Graham, Nottingham University, 1988. Explains how people learn as adults and how teachers and tutors can teach more effectively.

- *Adults Learning*, Jennifer Rogers, Open University Press, 1989. An established handbook, giving down-to-earth advice on all the common problems of helping adults learn.

- *Learning Skills Resource Bank*, National Extension College, 1989. Fifty copyright-free activities designed to help individual learners develop the study methods that suit them best.

- *Promoting Active Learning*, Penny Henderson, National Extension College, 1989. Explains how to involve learners more fully and promote effective group learning. Includes photocopiable sheets.

- *Teaching Adults*, Alan Rogers, Open University Press, 1986. Looks at all the key issues involved in teaching adults as opposed to other groups of students.

- *Use Your Head*, Tony Buzan, BBC Publications, 1989 (revised edition). Invaluable advice on effective study methods.

Conclusion

It is only too apparent that retirement today has become a much more varied and complex stage of life. No longer a short period following a long working life in the same industry or career, it now requires active planning and preparation for an extended third stage of life that may start earlier and last longer for more people than ever before.

Although the material resources that equip people for this life-stage still vary widely, the opportunity to think and plan for the future can be of practical help and of long-standing value. A period of life when employment is no longer the dominant activity or focus entails both highs and lows. It involves both greater freedoms and restrictions, gains and losses.

This book has attempted to encourage an understanding of retirement — both the event and the period of life — and to offer practical suggestions for helping employees with retirement pre-paration. The emphasis must always be on discovering what is helpful to offer people, and providing it in the most effective way.

Further information

∎ Useful addresses

Action Resource Centre
102 Park Village East
London NW1 3SP
Tel: 071-383 2200

**Age Exchange Theatre
Company**
11 Blackheath Village
Blackheath
London SE3 9LA
Tel: 071-318 9105

**Association for
Educational Gerontology**
c/o Centre for Social
Gerontology
Department of Applied
Social Studies
University of Keele
Staffs ST5 5VG
Tel: 0782 621111

**British Association for
Counselling**
1 Regent Place
Rugby CV21 2PJ
Tel: 0788 578328

**British Association for
Services to the Elderly**
119 Hassell Street
Newcastle under Lyme
Staffs ST5 1AX
Tel: 0782 661033

**Centre for Health and
Retirement Education**
Nodus Centre
University Campus
Guildford
Surrey GU2 5RX
Tel: 0483 39350

**Centre for Policy on
Ageing**
25-31 Ironmonger Row
London EC1V 3QP
Tel: 071-253 1787

**City and Guilds of London
Institute**
76 Portland Place
London W1N 4AA
Tel: 071-278 2468

**Commission for Racial
Equality**
Elliot House
10-12 Allington Street
London SW1E 5EH
Tel: 071-828 7022

**Department of Social
Security (DSS)**
FREEPHONE to order
leaflets 0800 666555
9.00am-4.30pm Mon-Fri

**Employers' Retirement
Association**
c/o Vickers plc
Millbank Tower
London SW1P 4RA
Tel:071-828 7777

**Financial Intermediaries,
Managers & Brokers
Regulatory Association
(FIMBRA)**
Hertsmere House
Hertsmere Road
London E14 4AB
Tel: 071-538 8860

**Health Education
Authority**
Hamilton House
Mabledon Place
London WC1H 9TX
Tel: 071-383 3833

The Industrial Society
Peter Runge House
3 Carlton House Terrace
London SW1 5DG
Tel: 071-839 4300

**Institute of Personnel
Management**
35 Camp Road
London SW19 4UX
Tel: 081-946 9100

**Investment Management
Regulatory Organisation
(IMRO)**
Broadwalk House
5 Appold Street
London EC2A 2LL
Tel: 071-628 6022

**Life Assurance & Unit
Trust Regulatory
Organisation (LAUTRO)**
Centre Point
103 New Oxford Street
London WC1A 1QH
Tel: 071-379 0444

**Money Management
Council**
18 Doughty Street
London WC1N 2PL
Tel: 071-405 1985

National Extension College
18 Brooklands Avenue
Cambridge CB2 2HN
Tel: 0223 316644

National Institute of Adult Continuing Education (NIACE)
19B De Montfort Street
Leicester LE1 7GE
Tel: 0533 551451

Open University (OU)
Walton Hall
Milton Keynes MK7 6AG
Tel: 0908 653231
(answering service 0908 652805)

Pre-Retirement Association
Nodus Centre
University Campus
Guildford
Surrey GU2 5RX
Tel: 0483 39323/39350

Registrar of Pension Schemes
PO Box 1NN
Newcastle upon Tyne NE99 1NN

RELATE
Herbert Gray College
Little Church Street
Rugby
Warwickshire CV21 3AP
Tel: 0788 573241

Retired Executives Action Clearing House (REACH)
89 Southwark Street
London SE1 OHD
Tel: 071-928 0452

University of London
Birkbeck College
Centre for Extra Mural Studies
26 Russell Square
London WC1B 5DQ
Tel: 071-636 8000

University of Surrey
Department of
Educational Studies
Guildford
Surrey GU2 5XH
Tel: 0483 300800 ext 9189

Workers' Educational Association (WEA)
Temple House
9 Upper Berkeley Street
London W1H 8BY
Tel: 071-402 5608

Recommended reading

Research reports

- *The Impact of Pre-Retirement Education: A Longitudinal Evaluation*, C Phillipson and P Strang, Department of Adult Education, University of Keele, 1983.

- *Preparation for Retirement in England and Wales*, Allin Coleman, National Institute of Adult Education and the Pre-Retirement Association, 1982.

- *Preparation for Retirement in Europe: The preserve of the privileged few?*, Maggie Pearson, John Lansley and Kathy Pick, Journal of Educational Gerontology (Vol 4, No 2, October 1989), Association for Educational Gerontology (address on p 113).

Practical help for planners

- *Coping with Change: Focus on Retirement*, Allin Coleman & Anthony Chiva, Health Education Authority, 1991. Resource materials for mid-life and pre-retirement programmes. Available from PRA (address on p 115).

- *Health and Retirement: An Ideas and Resources Pack for Health Educators*, Centre for Health and Retirement Education, 1986. Includes 10 units of training materials and 4 short videos. Available from CHRE (address on p 113).

- *Planning Retirement*, Open University short course in the Community Education series. Study Pack, Assessment Pack, Complete Course. Contact Open University (address on p 115).

- *The PRA's Manual of Pre-Retirement Education*, John Lumbard *et al*, Pre-Retirement Association in cooperation with Choice Magazine Company, 1990 (2nd edition). Available from Choice Publications, Apex House, Oundle Road, Peterborough PE2 9NP.

- *Retirement Counselling – A practical guide for action*, Harold Riker and Jane Myers, Hemisphere Publishing Corporation (USA), 1990.

- *What Next? — Focus on Health*, Centre for Health and Retirement Education, 1987. Booklet on retirement health, can be used as a course handout. Available to course leaders only, from CHRE (address on p 113).

Other books/reports for planners

- *The Best is Yet to Come — A workbook for early retirement*, Maggie Smith, Lifeskills Associates, 1989. Available from Lifeskills Associates, 51 Clarendon Road, Leeds LS2 9NZ.
- *Early Retirement*, Ann E McGoldrick and Cary L Cooper, Gower, 1988.
- *Practical Counselling and Helping Skills*, Richard Nelson Jones, Cassell Educational Ltd, 1988.
- *The Time of our Life: Education, Employment and Retirement in the Third Age*, Tom Schuller and Alan Walker, Institute for Public Policy Research, 1990.

Older adults — teaching and learning

- *Adult and Continuing Education*, Peter Jarvis, Routledge, 1988.
- *Adult Learning Strategies and Approaches: Resources for teachers of adults*, John Cummings *et al*, National Institute of Adult Continuing Education (NIACE), 1987.
- *Adults in Education*, Jennifer Rogers (ed), BBC Publications, 1989 (revised edition).
- *Learning Later: A handbook for developing educational opportunities with older people*, Unit for Development of Adult Continuing Education and Open University, 1988.
- *Older Learners — The Challenge of Adult Education*, Susanna Johnston and Chris Phillipson (eds), Bedford Square Press and Help the Aged, 1983.
- *Running Informal Learning Groups*, M Lever *et al*, National Extension College, 1985.

- *Tutor's Toolkit: An open learning resource for first time tutors*, Rosemary Napper and Dianna Batchelor, National Extension College, 1989.

Packages on pre-retirement education

- *The Choice Retirement Briefing File — New Choices*. Loose-leaf binder divided into sections offering advice for planning a successful retirement. File with 12 months subscription to *Choice Magazine*; discounts for quantity orders. Contact Choice, Apex House, Oundle Road, Peterborough PE2 9NP.

- *Comfort Zones: Planning your future (a practical guide for retirement planning)*, C Corbett and N Urquhart, Crisp Publications, 1990 (second edition). Workbook plus leader's guide. Available from Crisp Publications, 95 First Street, Los Altos, California CA 94022.

- *Planning Retirement* (Open University Course). Study Pack, Assessment Pack, Complete Course. Contact Open University (address on p 115).

'Popular' books on retirement

- *Good Retirement Guide*, R Brown, Bloomsbury Publishing Ltd (updated annually).

- Letts Retirement Guides: *Good Health*, Dr Edward Burgess; *Finance*, Douglas Shields; *Leisure and Travel*, Audrey Colville; *House and Garden*, Grace Shackleton. Charles Letts & Co, 1986.

- *Many Happy Retirements*, P Schweitzer, Age Exchange Theatre Company, 1988 (address on p 113).

- *The Mid-Career Action Guide*, Derek and Fred Kemp, Kogan Page, 1991.

- Saga Guides: *Food Guide*, Carol Leverkus; *Health Guide*, Dr Muir Gray; *Leisure Guide*, Roy Johnstone; *Money Guide*, Paul Lewis; *Rights Guide*, Paul Lewis; *Property Guide*, Michael Dineen. Unwin Hyman Ltd, 1988.

- *The Time of Your Life*, Help the Aged in association with the Health Education Authority, 1988.

Journals and newsletters

- *Adults Learning*, National Institute of Adult Continuing Education (NIACE). Monthly/annual subscription. (NIACE, address on p 115).

- *Ageing and Society*, Centre for Policy on Ageing and the British Society of Gerontology, Cambridge University Press.

- *Choice Magazine*. Monthly from booksellers/annual subscription from publisher. Also available as part of PRA membership. (Choice Publications, Apex House, Oundle Road, Peterborough PE2 9NP.)

- *FREE Information Bulletin*, Forum on the Rights of Elderly People to Education (FREE). Quarterly/annual subscription. (FREE c/o Age Concern England, address on p 151.)

- *Information Circular*. Monthly from Age Concern England, annual subscription.

- *Journal of Educational Gerontology*, Association for Educational Gerontology (AEG). Two parts per year (address on p 113).

- *PRA Resources Unit News*, free to PRA members (non-member subscription available), quarterly. (PRA Resources Unit, address on p 115.)

■ Bibliography

Chapter 1

Bixby, L, 'Retirement Patterns in the United States' in *Social Security Bulletin*, Vol 39, August 1976.

Central Statistical Office, *Social Trends 20*, HMSO, 1990.

Chapman, E N, *Comfort Zones: Planning your future (a practical guide for retirement planning)*, Crisp Publications, 1990 (2nd edition), pp 39–43.

Coleman, A and Chiva, A, *Coping with Change: Focus on Retirement*, Health Education Authority and Centre for Health and Retirement Education, 1991.

Department of Social Security, *Options for Equality in State Pension Age*, HMSO, 1991.

Glendenning, F and Fru, F, *Black and Ethnic Minority Elders: Retirement Issues*, Pre-Retirement Association, 1990.

Lumbard, J *et al*, *The PRA's Manual of Pre-Retirement Education*, Pre-Retirement Association in cooperation with Choice Magazine Company, 1986.

Chapter 2

Brown, R, *IPM Factsheet 35*, Institute of Personnel Management, 1990.

Chapman, E N, *Comfort Zones: Planning your future (a practical guide for retirement planning)*, Crisp Publications, 1990 (2nd edition), p 39.

Legal & General Assurance, *Survey*, GALLUP, 1989.

Lumbard, J *et al*, *The PRA's Manual of Pre-Retirement Education*, Pre-Retirement Association in cooperation with Choice Magazine Company, 1986.

Plett, P, *Training of Older Workers in Industrialised Countries*, International Labour Office, 1990.

Working Out, Spring 1991, p 7.

Chapter 3

Heron, A, *Solving New Problems*, Institute of Directors, 1959.

Chapter 4

Coleman, A and Chiva, A, *Coping with Change: Focus on Retirement*, Health Education Authority and Centre for Health and Retirement Education, 1991, p 7.

Diploma in the Practice of Education, University of Surrey Department of Educational Studies, 1990.

Gilbert, H, *Experiences of Learning Together*, PRA Resources Unit News Supplement, 1991.

Heron, A, *Solving New Problems*, Institute of Directors, 1959.

Lumbard, J *et al*, *The PRA's Manual of Pre-Retirement Education*, Pre-Retirement Association in cooperation with Choice Magazine Company, 1986, p 7.

Monitoring, Evaluation and Review — The QA framework for short courses at the University of Bath, University of Bath.

Options Pre-Retirement Services and Mid-Life Planning Associates, joint statement about curriculum design practice (unpublished).

Pre-Retirement Association, *Women and Retirement Seminar Report*, PRA, 1990.

School Science Review, 1985, vol 66, pp 645–650.

Toulson, N, *Preparing Staff for Retirement*, Gower, 1987.

Wilcox, J, *Years Ahead: Broadcasting and the educational needs of the elderly*, Independent Broadcasting Authority, 1984.

Chapter 5

British Broadcasting Corporation, *Adults in Education*, 1984, pp 68, 76–79.

Centre for Health and Retirement Education, *Health and Retirement: Ideas and Resources Pack*, 1986, Units 2 and 8.

Chapman, E N, *Comfort Zones: Planning your future (a practical guide for retirement planning)*, Crisp Publications, 1990 (2nd edition).

Napper, R and Batchelor, D, *Tutor's Toolkit: An open learning resource for first time tutors*, National Extension College, 1989, p34.

National Institute of Adult Continuing Education, *Yearbook*, 1991/92, pp 31–35.

Appendix 1

Excerpt from integrated policy statement and programme from Leyland DAF

Policy: Planning for retirement POLICY NO 7.5

4 General principles

The Company regards as very important the preparation of its employees for their retirement. The years following giving up full-time employment can be made richer and more enjoyable if proper thought and planning is devoted to the anticipated problems in plenty of time. It is important that the Company's approach to ways in which employees can be helped in this way is as consistent as can be across the Company, given limitations imposed by the different resources, internal and external, at different Company locations.

Provisions under this policy should be regarded as a normal benefit, available to any employee who wishes to take advantage of it.

5 Benefits

5.1 **Retirement planning seminars**
These should be in two sessions, Part A and Part B.

5.1.1 PART A The purpose of this is to prepare employees in good time for some of the changes likely to take place when they retire. Part A should be available to employees at between 5 and 6 years before expected retirement and should, if possible, where organised internally, contain appropriate treatment of the appropriate elements either in a written hand-out or by lecture/discussion/group sessions, etc.

5.1.2 PART B This is intended to enhance employees' awareness of the different ways in which years following retirement can be enriched so that natural apprehension can be allayed. The seminar should also provide basic technical information regarding benefits, etc and should be available during the 12 months prior to retirement.

5.2 Hard/copy material

As a complement to the Retirement Planning Seminars, employees should be provided, when they leave, with one of the 'Retirement Packs' produced by major publishing companies (eg Home and Law Publishing's 'Retirement Pack' or Choice Magazine's 'Retirement Planning File'). In any case, these should be available to individuals who choose not to attend the Seminars. Supplies of this material can be coordinated centrally to save cost.

5.3 Club membership

Membership of the '050 Club' should be offered to employees at 5–6 years prior to retirement, at initial cost to the Company. Membership entitles employees to newsletters, a regular magazine, telephone help-lines and vouchers for free or cheap goods or services.

5.4 Plant treatment

At the point of retirement, the employee should be able to join the Plant or Function Director for a cup of coffee and a chance to say 'thank you' and wish the employee well. If a spouse or partner exists, they should receive flowers or a tankard.

5.5 Pension

Immediately prior to Part B of the Retirement Planning Seminar, employees should receive a Pension Benefit Quotation, and appropriate counselling from the Pensions Administrator.

5.6 Medical

Retiring employees should be able to request a medical check by the Company's local Medical Adviser. His advice should be sought as to what standard of check is appropriate in the circumstances.

5.7 General

Retirement is more often than not a stage of life which is at least begun with a life partner. It is important that preparation for retirement is undertaken jointly and for this reason employees should be invited to bring their spouses or other partners to the Retirement Planning Seminars.

5.8 Self-help

Notwithstanding all the above, one of the objects of planning for retirement is to develop a degree of independence, where that does not already exist. Assistance from the Company should not be interpreted as 'spoonfeeding' and the Planning Seminars should each contain significant opportunities for employees to express their own needs and their own ideas for satisfying these needs.

In addition, it should not be assumed that all seminars should be entirely in Company time. Where tutorial resources permit, content should be allowed to extend into the evening, for instance.

Also, although the Company will fund the supply of retirement 'packs' (see para 5.2), the employee will be expected to pay for annual updating material and also to pay annual subscriptions to appropriate organisations where he wishes to remain a member.

6 Action Following Retirement

In some locations, organisations of retired employees are well organised and active. In others they do not exist at all. For this reason, it is not appropriate to expect a consistent Company policy on post-retirement assistance to exist across the country. However, it is important that some facility exists for ex-employees of the Company (Leyland DAF) to receive advice and counselling when they encounter personal difficulties. This may simply mean Personnel Departments having local contacts in welfare organisations and state benefits offices.

7 Procedures

Within each location, the organisation of retirement planning is the responsibility of the personnel function. Whatever personnel information computer system is in use at the location should be used to generate regular listings of employees reaching the relevant age within the coming twelve months, and retirement planning action taken accordingly. No employee within the appropriate age range should be omitted from the provisions of this policy, except at his or her own wish.

Attendance at the Planning Seminars should always be logged on the location's personnel information computer system and regular audits carried out to ensure that employees are not missed inadvertently.

Where retirements occur unexpectedly (in cases of redundancy, for instance), appropriate arrangements should be made for those people who have not had the opportunity of attending Part A. This would involve combining the contents of Parts A and B.

Pensions Administrators, acting from the retirement listings, should be sure that Estimated Quotation Requests are submitted to the Company's Pensions Administrators in plenty of time, so that retiring employees receive a quotation early enough to enable them to voice queries with the Plant Pensions Administrator or at the Retirement Seminar.

Personnel Departments are also responsible for ensuring that appointments are made for the retiring employees and their Director, and for arranging the appropriate gift to be delivered to the retiring employee's partner (see para 5.4).

Personnel Departments must also ensure that a medical appointment is made at a reasonable interval before retirement (see para 5.6).

Locations which are obviously too small to resource any or all of the above must take the responsibility of making suitable arrangements with a 'parent' location with greater resources.

Appendix 2

Excerpt from *Divisional Personnel Manual*, Scottish Health Service Common Services Agency

Preparation for retirement

Principles

General Whitley Council

1 The General Whitley Council Handbook Section 55 refers and recommends that Employing Authorities provide reasonable facilities to enable all employees within a minimum of 12 months service with NHS and who are within 2 years of their expected retirement date to make proper preparation for their retirement from the service.

2 Wherever reasonable, subject to prior approval, special leave with pay should be given for employees to attend a Preparation for Retirement course organised by the Employing Authority and/or by the local Education Authority.

3 Individual counselling facilities should also be made available to employees, where there is a need for this.

4 Information on the NHS Retirement Fellowship should be made available to all employees.

Procedure

1 Preparation for retirement

a SENIOR STAFF The Welfare Officer, Trinity Park House, will be responsible to the General Manager for administration of staff retirals related to non-delegated posts, eg directors of divisions, staff reporting to the directors.

b OTHER STAFF The Divisional Officer with Personnel Responsibility will be responsible to his/her Director of Division for the administration of staff retirals in the Division.

2 Information packages/other advice/assistance/support

The Welfare Officer, Trinity Park House, maintains up to date information on all aspects of Retirement and will assist Divisional Officers with Personnel Responsibility in providing support back-up as required.

Date	Action to be taken	By
2 years prior to employee reaching retirement age	Identification of employees due to reach retiree age or over during next 2 years.	Welfare Officer
	Forward plan retirement seminars based on number/location and circulate notices to all Divisions.	Central Personnel Training Section
	Advise Divisions of those staff identified as approaching retirement age within next 2 years.	Welfare Officer
	Contact employee newly identified to offer advice/assistance and to identify expected retirement date.	Divisional Officer with Personnel Responsibility
	Plan for attendance at in-house seminars.	Same as above
	Complete reference sheet	Welfare Officer
	Obtain retirement information package for those who wish to attend in-house seminars. Liaise with Line Manager.	Divisional Officer with Personnel Responsibility

Date	Action to be taken	By
Regular basis throughout the year	Hold seminars.	Welfare Officer
	Offer individual counselling.	Welfare Officer
1 year prior to employee retiral date	Agree employee annual leave arrangements to ensure that any leave due is taken.	Line Manager
4-6 months prior to employee retiral date	Prepare employee letter for signature by Director of Division.	Divisional Officer
	Assist in completion of employment documentation. Forward paperwork to Salaries & Wages Department.	Divisional Officer
	Plan final day, eg retiral presentation.	Director of Division

Appendix 3

From Scottish Health Service Common Services Agency

Sample letter to employee within the NHS

Dear

PREPARATION FOR RETIREMENT
Our records show that you are approaching a
time when you are possibly beginning to
consider retirement from work. As you know,
the normal retirement age is 65 years but
those aged 60 or over who are members of the
NHS Superannuation Scheme may receive their
NHS Pension at any time from age 60.

If, therefore, you are considering retiring
from work within the next two years, you may
be interested in attending one of our one-day
'in-house' Preparation for Retirement
seminars designed to briefly outline issues
regarding pension payments, financial
investment, health, fitness and increased
leisure time. Time off with pay will be given
to employees who wish to attend Preparation
for Retirement courses. An opportunity can
also be given to attend an external pre-
retirement course in your home area, if you
so wish, and our Divisional Officer with
Personnel Responsibility on extension ... can
provide further information on this matter
and on any other aspect you may wish to raise.

I appreciate that you may not be retiring for
some time yet but this letter is to alert you
to the support and assistance that can be
provided to help you plan your retirement. It
would be useful, therefore, if you could
indicate your planned year of retirement to
..., Divisional Officer with Personnel
Responsibility.

With best wishes.
Yours sincerely

Director of Division

Sample letter to employee who does not wish to attend in-house course

Dear

PREPARATION FOR RETIREMENT
I note that you are not interested in attending an in-house Preparation for Retirement seminar and I therefore thought you might find the enclosed information helpful.

May I also remind you that if you wish to attend an external Preparation for Retirement course, you should contact me again so that I may process this on your behalf and arrange for approval by the Director of Division of time off with pay and reasonable expenses.

With best wishes.
Yours sincerely

Divisional Officer with Personnel Responsibility
cc Line Manager

Sample letter offering assistance after retiral date

Dear

PREPARATION FOR RETIREMENT

I refer to your notified retiral date of ... and write to offer the services of our Divisional Officer with Personnel Responsibility who would be pleased to assist you in the completion and procession of the necessary paperwork at this time. Please ring ... on ext ... who will be happy to help you in this way.

May I also remind you that Mrs ..., our Welfare Officer, based at ..., tel ... ext ..., will be happy to discuss with you any matters on retirement about which you are unsure. Please ring her to arrange a suitable appointment if you so wish.

If I can assist you further, please do not hesitate to contact me.

Meanwhile, may I take this opportunity to extend my warm thanks to you for your years of excellent service and to wish you a long and happy retirement.

With best wishes.
Yours sincerely

Director of Division
cc Staff Welfare Officer
Line Manager

Appendix 4

Example of a pre-course questionnaire from Bristol Folk House
(Adult Education Centre)

Retirement planning

A time to look forward

This questionnaire is to help you think about some of the course topics
before joining us at Folk House. It would help us if you would return it
before the course commences, or even on the first day.

Please tick the relevant column.

Question	Strongly agree	Agree	Neutral	Disagree	Strongly disagree
1 I think that retirement is a time of moving from dependence to independence.	☐	☐	☐	☐	☐
2 I believe that life after work is a time of growth.	☐	☐	☐	☐	☐

Question	Strongly agree	Agree	Neutral	Disagree	Strongly disagree
3 My health will not be a major preoccupation in my life after work.	☐	☐	☐	☐	☐
4 I think it essential to take up a new activity in my life after work.	☐	☐	☐	☐	☐
5 I am sure that the stress factor will significantly reduce when I leave work.	☐	☐	☐	☐	☐
6 Finance will not be a major concern in my life after work.	☐	☐	☐	☐	☐
7 Retirement planning is important for people at least five years before leaving work.	☐	☐	☐	☐	☐

Question	Strongly agree	Agree	Neutral	Disagree	Strongly disagree
8 I look forward to attending the Retirement Planning Course.	☐	☐	☐	☐	☐
9 I believe I will not learn anything new on the course.	☐	☐	☐	☐	☐

10 Please insert a topic that you would like discussed on the course.

The topic I would like included is:

_____

Thank you for helping us with this questionnaire.

Appendix 5

Example 1 from Ford Motor Company Ltd, Welfare & Benefits Employee Services course

Example 2 from Workers' Educational Association, Thames and Solent

Example 3 from Workers' Educational Association

Samples of programmes

Example 1 **Mid-life planning: going forward from Ford (2 day programme)**

Programme Seminar for Senior Managers and their Partners 16–18 December 1991 at Wivenhoe Park Conference Centre and Hotel, University of Essex, Colchester.

Welcome Here is the Outline Agenda; on the succeeding pages you will find much more detail.

Mid-Life Adjustment and Thinking about Change

State Benefits and Rights

Change and Living Circumstances

The Ford Occupational Pension

Optional Sessions: An Early Morning Walk, The National Trust, Holidays and High Days

Time Management: An Active Life

Feeling Good, Food, Relaxation

Being Fit: Look After Yourself

Men and Women Facing Change

Time Management: Leisure and Learning Interest

Money Management: Savings, Investment, Income

Enclosed A three-part questionnaire to help focus the sessions on Pensions, Money Management and State Benefits. If you send this to the Course Director it will be treated in confidence, but assist him greatly in the planning of the sessions, making them particularly relevant for your needs.

Example 2 Workers' Educational Association, Thames & Solent (3 day programme)

Preparation for retirement

18, 19, 20 February 1991 9.00 am–4.30 pm

At the Staff Training Centre, Crowthorne, Berkshire

Monday 18 February	9.00–10.15	Approaching Retirement *P Hartley*
	10.15	Coffee
	10.30–12.30	Health in Retirement *M Deacock*
	12.30	Lunch
	1.30–2.30	Insurance *D Rose, ABI*
	2.30–4.30	NHS Pensions Scheme *In-house speaker*
Tuesday 19 February	9.00–10.15	Lifestyle Changes *P Hartley*
	10.15	Coffee
	10.30–12.00	DSS Pensions and Benefits *Mrs B Bracknell*
	12.00–12.30	The Retirement Home *P Hartley*
	12.30	Lunch
	1.30–2.30	Changing Relationships *P Hartley*
	2.30–4.30	Financial Planning *I Sharp, Frizzells*
Wednesday 20 February	9.00–10.00	Security in the Home *Mrs B Bracknell*
	10.15	Coffee
	10.30–11.30	Occupation and Recreation *P Hartley*
	11.30–12.30	Home, Routine, Money *P Hartley*
	·12.30	Lunch
	1.30–2.00	Occupation and Recreation (cont) *P Hartley*
	2.00–3.00	Making a Will *G Green*
	3.00–4.30	Summary and Evaluation *P Hartley*
		Course Tutor *Peter Hartley*
		Course Co-ordinator *Mick Pither*

Example 3   **Workers' Educational Association
(1 week programme)**
CSS (PSA) 75 Preparation for Retirement
Thursdays, 25 October–6 December 10.30am–4.15pm
(1 November 2.00–4.15pm)
Building B, Government Offices, Coley Park, Reading

Thursday 25 October	2.00–4.15	Approaching Retirement *G Clarke*
Thursday 1 November	10.30–11.30	Lifestyle Changes: Home & Routine *G Clarke*
	11.30–12.30	Money Matters *G Clarke*
	1.30–3.30	Financial Planning *M O'Sullivan*
	3.30–4.15	Occupations in Retirement *G Clarke*
Thursday 8 November	2.00–4.00	Health in Retirement *V Chatterton*
	3.30–4.15	Round-up *G Clarke*
Thursday 15 November	2.00–3.30	DSS Pensions *DSS Reading*
	3.30–4.15	Voluntary work *G Clarke*
Thursday 22 November	2.00–4.15	Recreation and Leisure *G Clarke*
Thursday 29 November	2.00–3.00	Security in the Home *Sergeant Sugg*
	3.00–4.15	Changing Relationships *G Clarke*
Thursday 6 December	2.00–3.00	Making a Will *J Deering*
	3.00–4.15	Summary and Evaluation *G Clarke*
		Course Tutor *G Clarke*
		Course Co-ordinator *C Higgs*

Appendix 6

Example 1 from Money Management Council

Example 2 abridged from Workers' Educational Association, Thames & Solent (S Grylls, 1987)

Examples of briefings for contributors to programmes

Example 1 **Excerpt from voluntary code of practice for visiting tutors on money matters**

The visiting tutor's role

a The visiting tutor should help the group to understand the principles of money management in relation to each individual's personal circumstances, intentions and needs.

b No attempt may be made to offer individual financial advice in the educational group setting.

c Illustrations and suggestions should be made in generic and comparative terms, showing the kind of services and products to be obtained from a bank, a building society, an insurance company, a unit trust manager, etc.

d No specific reference may be made to the tutor's own products or services, and neither they nor any other specific company product or service may be recommended.

e Detailed and technical information should be carefully limited to the expressed needs of the group at the relevant point in their explorations, and/or when appropriate in the judgement of the group leader. Otherwise, if the visiting tutor attempts to give out detailed technical information, the session will be difficult to digest and the details will be irrelevant to the individual circumstances of many on the course.

Example 2   Tips for specialist speakers

The first major point, especially for inexperienced speakers is DON'T WORRY too much. By far the majority of participants on these courses want to like you, enjoy your session and learn from you, and the tutor will have made efforts to create a friendly, co-operative atmosphere in sessions before you arrive.

Find out who your audience is

You need to think what you need to know about the participants — age ? marital status ? health ? etc. You can find this out by several routes.

Introduce yourself

Explain who you are, where you fit into the professional grouping for your subject. Then explain what you intend to cover during the session — people feel safer and can understand better if they know your plan.

It also helps to say whether you want them to interrupt as you go along, or whether there will be a discussion period — which should be about as long as the 'delivery'.

Plan flexibility

You can't possibly cover all your topic in the time allocated — even if you could, the students couldn't take it in. Therefore look on your session as an opportunity to: raise the important questions; point out where more information is available; relate your topic to people's circumstances.

Variety

Few people can listen profitably for more than 20 minutes at a stretch — try to alter the pace. One very useful skill to acquire is that of asking open-ended questions which can elicit ideas, instantaneous evaluation, or thoughtful responses to issues you may have raised. Other methods you might adopt are:

a   Setting the group a 'problem' and asking them what they'd do or what they know. This could be done in small groups or in the large group.

b   Ask one or two questions and get people to work out their needs (eg what I do to ensure I stay healthy; changes I could make in my diet; my major financial worries, etc). This could be done in the large group or in pairs, threes, etc.

c If your subject is issue-based, ask participants to discuss an issue in groups and report back. NB Don't try to reach unanimity — one of the features of preparing for retirement is that people should feel OK about their own style.

d Set exercises in which students have to 'find their way' around your topic.

Remember that a two hour session *must* have a break in it, even if it is just for leg-stretching.

Audio-visual aids
Seeing facts, particularly numbers, helps people to understand and remember.

a Blackboards, whiteboards and flipcharts are excellent for temporarily highlighting what you or the group are saying.

b OHPs and flipcharts are good for pre-prepared information. A useful guide is to have no more than 8 words across and 8 lines down.

c If using films, slides or audio tapes, remember not everyone can see or hear perfectly.

NB Too much a/v material can confuse or overload. Always explain an a/v presentation and allow time for questions and discussion.

Timekeeping
There is usually room for flexibility about this and you shouldn't feel too bound to fill exactly 1 or 2 hours as the case may be. On the other hand, other speakers may be timetabled to follow immediately after you. Discuss this with the tutor beforehand.

Contact with tutors
We are encouraging tutors and speakers to make contact before the course: be sure to discuss a) who the students are b) any audio-visual equipment you need c) the content of your session d) any requirements about room layout.

Appendix 7

Example of post-course questionnaire from Pam Duveen
(Consultant)

Programme evaluation questionnaire

Feedback form

We would be grateful if you could complete this form giving us your honest
response to the course. Please add any additional comments you care to
make.

Item	Was it relevant?	Have you found it helpful?	Comments
Objectives and introduction to the course			
State Pension and benefits			
Income Tax & other tax matters			

Planning your financial future			
Time on your hands			
Pension			

1 Were there any topics which you felt should be shortened in duration or completely omitted from the course? (If so, please state which topics and why.)

_____

_____

2 Do you think we should have included any other topics or spent more time on certain areas?

_____

3 Have you any other suggestions on ways in which the course might be improved for the future?

_____

4 Is there anything you would like to follow on from this course (eg meetings, further information, etc)?

_____

5 What is your overall opinion of the course? (please circle appropriate choice)
a Weak
b Only satisfactory (room for much improvement)
c Average
d Good (minor points of detail could be improved)
e Very beneficial (time well spent)

Signed (only if you wish)   Date

Appendix 8

Example of a self-assessment questionnaire from *Tutor's Toolkit: An open learning resource for first time tutors*, D Batchelor and R Napper, National Extension College, 1989, p 74

YOUR STRENGTHS AS A TUTOR

Think of yourself in your role as a tutor.
Think of an example or incident relating to yourself in that role recently.
What skills/knowledge/attitudes and approaches did you use?

1 _____ 4 _____

2 _____ 5 _____

3 _____ 6 _____

What skills/knowledge/attitudes would have been useful that you didn't have?

1 _____ 4 _____

2 _____ 5 _____

3 _____ 6 _____

Circle the three most important of these. How could you go about acquiring them? Now tick the statements below and try to identify definite steps you can take.

☐ Books about teaching or about your subject. Where could you find them?

☐ Practice. How would you know you had improved?

☐ Talking to others. When? How? What about?

☐ Other. What?

Appendix 9

Example of assessment for lecturer/speaker from *Adults in Education*, Jenny Rogers (ed), BBC Publications, 1984, p 69

QUESTIONNAIRE TO EVALUATE LECTURES

Surroundings and other factors
Please comment on any of the following (eg excessive, good, slight, poor . . .)

Noise	**Light**
Ventilation	**Space**
Seating	**Temperature**
Fatigue	**Hunger**

The lecture
VOICE

Audibility	☐ very clearly audible	☐ easily heard	☐ just audible
	☐ sometimes audible	☐ almost entirely inaudible	
Quality	☐ lively varied tone and pace	☐ fairly lively	☐ satisfactory
	☐ rather dull	☐ very monotonous	

| **Speed** | ☐ spoke much too fast | ☐ spoke rather quickly | ☐ about right |
| | ☐ spoke rather slowly | ☐ tediously slow | |

Comments, if any

| **Appearance and grooming** | ☐ very good — a pleasure to look at | ☐ good — a pleasing appearance on the whole | ☐ satisfactory |
| | ☐ rather poor | ☐ poor — disagreeable/ distracting | |

| **Manner** | ☐ very agreeable | ☐ pleasant | ☐ satisfactory |
| | ☐ rather disagreeable | ☐ unpleasant | |

| **Rapport with class** | ☐ excellent | ☐ good | ☐ satisfactory |
| | ☐ fair | ☐ poor | |

Comments, if any

CONTENT AND PRESENTATION

| **Amount of material** | ☐ far too much | ☐ rather too much | ☐ satisfactory |
| | ☐ rather little/ content thin | ☐ practically nothing worth saying | |

| **Clarity and organisation** | ☐ very clear/easy to follow | ☐ clear | ☐ only fairly clear |
| | ☐ rather difficult to follow — somewhat muddled | ☐ could not understand — less clear than before | |

Use	☐ will help me greatly in the future	☐ helpful	☐ of some use
	☐ practically no use	☐ absolutely no help	
Stimulus	☐ I shall certainly follow this up (by reading/practice)	☐ I shall probably follow this up	☐ I may follow this up
	☐ uninterested, would have been better occupied elsewhere	☐ very bored, shall avoid subject whenever possible, less interested than before	

Comments, if any _____

AUDIO-VISUAL MATERIALS

Board/screens	☐ material very clearly and attractively presented	☐ material well presented	☐ satisfactory
	☐ untidy, rather crowded, partly illegible	☐ almost illegible	
Slides or other visual illustration	☐ very clear and attractive	☐ well presented	☐ satisfactory
	☐ lettering too· small, slides rather crowded	☐ almost illegible	
Sound	☐ very clear and agreeable	☐ clear	☐ satisfactory
	☐ not entirely audible	☐ almost inaudible	

Comments, if any _____

About the Pre-Retirement

Association

The Pre-Retirement Association of Great Britain and Northern Ireland is the major organisation within the country promoting awareness of the needs of all those preparing for retirement. Founded in 1964, the PRA provides education, planning and support services that relate to the successful management of transitional changes from an increasing diversity of employment patterns.

The PRA

- Works with people who help others through the preparation process that is mainly associated with the end of (full-time) paid employment, but which can begin from mid-life.

- Offers help and advice to employers, educators and voluntary bodies who are playing a part in people's retirement preparation, and wish to improve the support they offer.

- Runs courses and seminars for people approaching retirement through the Retirement Preparation Service, but does not advocate particular products or services.

- Is the national resource for information, ideas and the practice of retirement preparation. The PRA offers stimulus and support to those who provide services and activities as part of people's pre-retirement planning.

■ Has affiliated associations and development officers throughout the country who stimulate and coordinate interest in retirement preparation locally. These local associations may also provide services to members.

The PRA and its membership represent a national movement concerned with helping prepare for what is now recognised as the second half of adult life. Membership of the PRA allows you to draw on the wide variety of knowledge and experience in pre-retirement education, and to contribute to the support of others facing problems for the first time.

PRA publications

PRA Resources Unit News is a quarterly information bulletin covering news, views, new publications, events and short articles on topical issues in retirement preparation. A four-page pull out supplement gives a more in-depth coverage of professional matters for pre-retirement educators. Membership includes a copy of the News, but non-members may suscribe directly. Contact Resources Unit, Pre-Retirement Association.

The PRA Directory of Pre-Retirement Courses is an annual publication, listing course provision throughout the UK, in response to annual surveys. It covers courses in the commercial, educational and voluntary sector and gives standardised information on relevant course features, to enable comparison.

Your Retirement — PRA Retirement Course Notes is an annual A4 booklet giving basic details of the issues most commonly covered by courses run by the PRA for client companies, and distributed to delegates. Surplus supplies of the booklet are available for sale (£2.50 incl p+p).

The PRA Occasional Paper Series addresses topical issues for retirement planners. Current titles include:

Black & Ethnic Minority Elders: Retirement Issues

The Growth of Retirement Since 1951: A statistical view of the 50–74 age group

Pre-Retirement Education in the 1990s — The European Perspective

Flexibility in Retirement — Developing a Policy

Forthcoming titles

Work in Later Life

Sexuality in Later Life

Prices may vary, please enquire.

Information publications

Reading for Retirement (a reading list for retirees)

Introductory List for Educators

Professional Updating List

Audio-Visual Resources List

PRA Annual Report

To order publications, send a cheque or money order with invoice request to:

PRA, Nodus Centre, University Campus, Guildford, Surrey GU2 5RX.

About Age Concern

Preparing for Retirement: The employer's guide is one of a wide range of publications produced by Age Concern England — National Council on Ageing. In addition, Age Concern is actively engaged in training, information provision, research and campaigning for retired people and those who work with them. It is a registered charity dependent on public support for the continuation of its work.

Age Concern England links closely with Age Concern centres in Scotland, Wales and Northern Ireland to form a network of over 1,400 independent local UK groups. These groups, with the invaluable help of an estimated 250,000 volunteers, aim to improve the quality of life for older people and develop services appropriate to local needs and resources. These include advice and information, day care, visiting services, transport schemes, clubs, and specialist facilities for physically and mentally frail older people.

Age Concern England
1268 London Road
London SW16 4ER
Tel: 081-679 8000

Age Concern Wales
4th Floor
1 Cathedral Road
Cardiff CF1 9SD
Tel: 0222 371566

Age Concern Scotland
54A Fountainbridge
Edinburgh EH3 9PT
Tel: 031-228 5656

Age Concern Northern Ireland
6 Lower Crescent
Belfast BT7 1NR
Tel: 0232 245729

Publications from

 **Books**

A wide range of titles is published by Age Concern England under the ACE Books imprint.

Money Matters

Your Rights
Sally West
A highly acclaimed annual guide to the State Benefits available to older people. Contains current information on Income Support, Housing Benefit and Retirement Pensions, among other matters, and provides advice on how to claim.
Further information on application.

Using Your Home as Capital
Cecil Hinton
This best-selling book for home owners, which is updated annually, gives a detailed explanation of how to capitalise on the value of your home and obtain regular additional income.
Further information on application.

Your Taxes and Savings
Jennie Hawthorne and Sally West
Explains how the tax system affects people over retirement age, including how to avoid paying more tax than necessary. The information about savings covers the wide range of investment opportunities now available.
Further information on application.

Earning Money in Retirement
Kenneth Lysons
Many people, for a variety of reasons, wish to continue in some form of paid employment beyond the normal retirement age. This helpful guide explores the practical implications of such a choice and highlights some of the opportunities available.
£5.95 0-86242-103-9

General
Living, Loving and Ageing: Sexual and personal relationships in later life
Wendy Greengross and Sally Greengross
Sexuality is often regarded as the preserve of the younger generation. At last, here is a book for older people and those who work with them, which tackles the issues in a straightforward fashion, avoiding preconceptions and bias.
£4.95 0-86242-070-9

Health
Your Health in Retirement
Dr J A Muir Gray and Pat Blair
A comprehensive guide to help people look after their health. Full details are given of health advisers and useful organisations to contact for help.
£4.50 0-86242-082-2

Housing

Housing Options for Older People

David Bookbinder

A review of housing options is part of growing older. All the possibilities and their practical implications are carefully considered in this comprehensive guide.

£4.95 0-86242-108-x

To order books, send a cheque or money order to the address below: postage and packing is free. Credit card orders may be made on 081-679 8000.

ACE Books
Age Concern England
PO Box 9
London SW16 4EX

Information Factsheets

Age Concern England produces over 30 factsheets on a variety of subjects. Single copies are free on receipt of a 9″ x 6″ sae. If you require a selection of factsheets or multiple copies totalling more than 10, charges will be given on request.

A complete set of factsheets is available in a ring binder at the current cost of £32, which includes the first year's subscription. The current cost for annual subscription for subsequent years is £12. There are different rates of subscription for people living abroad.

Factsheets are revised and updated throughout the year and membership of the subscription service will ensure that your information is always current.

Write to the Information and Policy Department, Age Concern England, at the address given on page 151 for further information.

Index